New Directions: Efficiency and Productivity

Studies in Productivity and Efficiency

Series Editors:

Rolf Färe
Shawna Grosskopf
Oregon State University
R. Robert Russell
University of California, Riverside

Books in the series:

Fox, Kevin J.:
Efficiency in the Public Sector
Ball, V. Eldon and Norton, George W.:
Agricultural Productivity:
Measurement and Sources of Growth
Färe, Rolf and Grosskopf, Shawna:
New Directions:
Efficiency and Productivity

NEW DIRECTIONS: EFFICIENCY AND PRODUCTIVITY

ROLF FÄRE AND SHAWNA GROSSKOPF
Oregon State University

IN COLLABORATION WITH H. FUKUYAMA, W.F. LEE, W. WEBER AND O. ZAIM

Kluwer Academic Publishers
Boston/Dordrecht/London

Library of Congress Cataloging-in-Publication Data

Färe, Rolf, 1942-
New Directions: efficiency and productivity / Rolf Fare and Shawna Grosskopf in collaboration with H. Fukuyama, W. F. Lee, W. Weber ad O Zaim.
p. cm. (Studies in productivity and efficiency)
Includes bibliographical references and index.

1. Industrial efficiency. 2. Industrial Productivity. I. Grosskopf, Shawna. II. Title. III. Series.

ISBN 1-4020-7661-4 (HC)   ISBN 0-387-24963-X (SC)

Printed on acid-free paper

First softcover printing, 2005

Printed in the United States of America.

9 8 7 6 5 4 3 2 1   SPIN 11392484

springeronline.com

To
Björn Thalberg

Contents

List of Figures ix
Preface xi
Introduction xiii

1. ESSAY 1: EFFICIENCY INDICATORS AND INDEXES 1
   1 The Nerlovian Profit Indicator 2
   2 The Revenue Efficiency Indicator 13
   3 Cost Efficiency Indicator 22
   4 Efficiency Indexes 27
   5 From Indicators to Indexes 35
   6 Hyperbolic Efficiency 39
   7 Remarks on the Literature 42
   8 Appendix: Proofs 42

2. ESSAY 2: ENVIRONMENTAL PERFORMANCE 45
   1 Good and Bad Outputs 46
   2 Productivity with Bads 52
   3 Environmental Quantity Index 56
   4 Shadow Pricing Undesirable Outputs 60
   5 Property Rights and Profitability 65
      5.1 The Production Network with Externality 66
      5.2 Common-pool Resource Technology 70
      5.3 Property Rights, Profit and Externalities 71
      5.4 Profits and common pool resource 75
      5.5 Summary 77

6 Environmental Kuznets Curve 77
6.1 Methodology 79
6.2 Data and Results 82
6.3 Concluding Remarks 90
7 Remarks on the Literature 90
8 Appendix: Proofs 91

3. ESSAY 3: AGGREGATION ISSUES 93
1 The Fox Paradox 94
2 Koopmans' Theorem 96
3 Aggregating Indicators Across Firms 100
4 Johansen Aggregation 109
5 Aggregating Farrell Efficiency Indexes 115
6 Luenberger Productivity Indicators 119
7 Aggregation Across Inputs and Outputs 120
8 Aggregation and Decompositions 131
9 Performance in Japanese Banking 133
9.1 Introduction 133
9.2 The Japanese Banking System 134
9.3 Method 135
9.4 Data and Results 140
9.5 Summary 142
10 Remarks on the Literature 147
11 Appendix: Proofs 147

4. APPENDIX: AXIOMS OF PRODUCTION 151
1 Activity Analysis Model 157

Topic Index 169

Author Index 173

List of Figures

1.1	Profit Maximization	4
1.2	Directional Technology Distance Function	6
1.3	Efficiency and Direction Vectors	10
1.4	A Technology	11
1.5	Revenue Maximization	14
1.6	The Directional Output Distance Function	17
1.7	g_y-Efficiency	18
1.8	Decomposition of the Revenue Indicator	20
1.9	Cost Minimization	23
1.10	Relation Among Three Indicators	26
1.11	Input Distance Function	28
1.12	Farrell Input-Oriented Efficiency Indexes	29
1.13	Farrell Output Oriented Efficiency Indexes	34
1.14	The Directional Input Distance Function	37
1.15	Efficiency Inequalities	38
1.16	The Technology Hyperbolic Distance Function	40
2.1	Weak and Strong Disposability of Outputs	48
2.2	Directional output distance function with good and bad outputs	54
2.3	The Network Model with Externality	66
3.1	Koopmans' Theorem	98
3.2	The Revenue Aggregation Theorem	99
3.3	Johansen firm and industry production	112
3.4	Input Aggregation	123
3.5	The Industry Nerlovian Profit Efficiency Indicator (NI)	145

3.6 The Industry Luenberger Profitability Change Indicator (L) 146

4.1 Illustration of Proposition A.1 153

Preface

The format of this monograph is three essays, which we arrived at after spending a year writing over one hundred pages of what we eventually realized was a tedious reworking of old material. So we started over determined to write something new.

At first we thought this approach might not work as a coherent monograph, which is why we chose the essay format rather than chapters. As it turns out, there is a common thread—namely the directional distance function, which also gave us our title. As you shall see, the directional distance function includes traditional distance functions and efficiency measures as special cases providing a unifying framework for existing productivity and efficiency measures. It is also flexible enough to open up new areas in productivity and efficiency analysis such as environmental and aggregation issues. That we did not see this earlier is humbling; a student at a recent conference raised his hand and asked 'Why didn't you start with the directional distance function in the first place? Indeed. This manuscript is intended to make up for our earlier oversights.

This monograph contains papers coauthored with Wen-Fu Lee and Osman Zaim and one paper written by two former students, Hiroyuki Fukuyama and Bill Weber. We thank them for their contributions. Another former student, Jim Logan (Logi) read and critiqued the manuscript for which we are grateful.

Our students at Oregon State University worked through our essays; thanks are due to them for their diligence and patience. In the summer of 2001 Emili Grifell-Tatjé organized a workshop at The Autonomous University of Barcelona where we had the opportunity to present the main body of material in the manuscript. Thanks to Emili for this opportunity (and his generous hospitality) and the workshop participants for their valuable feedback.

Finally, as usual, we took advantage of Bert Balk's keen eye and asked him to go through the rough draft. Thank you again.

December 2004
Since this monograph first appeared we have had the opportunity to put it to the test with more of our students at Oregon State University. They were very vigilant and discovered a number of typographical errors. This fall we also had two visitors from Spain, Emili Tortosa-Ausina and Maria Teresa (Maite) Balaguer-Coll, who sat in on and helped teach our class and carefully read the manuscript, for which we thank them.

Introduction

The key unifying theme of this monograph is 'new directions'. It is literal in the broad sense that the monograph covers the new directions in which we are currently working in the general efficiency and productivity arena; it is literal in the more specific sense that the unifying conceptual tool is what we call the directional distance function. Nevertheless, we do keep our 'traditional' general approach to efficiency and productivity and its measurement—namely we start with axiomatic production theory and exploit the associated duality theory to derive our 'new' results.

Much of our previous work has promoted input and output distance functions as useful tools for modeling technologies with many inputs and outputs. These are defined as radial contractions or expansions of inputs and outputs, respectively. Under fairly general conditions these provide complete characterizations of technology, as well as having useful dual representations in the cost and revenue functions. Nevertheless, they have some limitations which arise from their 'radiality'.

One such limitation is that they do not readily provide duals to the profit function. Since they scale either on inputs or outputs but not both, the input and output distance functions do not provide a natural pairing with the profit function which does optimize over inputs and outputs simultaneously. Profit also has an additive structure—revenues minus costs—which is shared by the directional distance function but not the Shephard distance functions, which are multiplicative in form.

Another limitation of the traditional distance functions is revealed when we wish to model and measure performance when there is joint production of good (desirable) and bad (undesirable) outputs. The traditional output distance function would typically seek to expand the vector of both types of outputs, rather than crediting firms for reducing the undesirable outputs. The directional distance function can be customized to simultaneously seek expansions of desirable outputs and reductions in undesirable outputs.

Also, results to date concerning the aggregation properties of the traditional distance functions—either over firms to measure industry efficiency or over inputs and outputs to reduce dimensionality or accommodate limited data—are generally disappointing. As we shall see, the directional distance function serves to ameliorate this problem.

These issues are the basis of the new directions which we follow in this monograph, which is organized in three essays. The first takes up the specifics of the directional distance function as a generalization of the traditional distance functions. The directional distance function differs from the radial distance functions in that the former is defined with respect to a specific preassigned direction in which performance is evaluated. If this direction is taken to be observed inputs or outputs, the directional distance function is equivalent to the usual radial distance functions. The directional distance function literally provides new directions for performance measurement. This essay provides the general overarching basis for efficiency decompositions; the traditional cost and revenue efficiency measures and their components are special cases. Profit efficiency and productivity measured using the directional distance function introduces additive forms of performance measurement.

In the second essay we focus on environmental issues, where the directional distance function proves to be a very useful performance measure. In the last essay, we turn to issues in aggregation, where again the directional distance function proves to have favorable properties. Each of the last two essays includes applications. We have gathered the basic axioms of production employed throughout the monograph in a final appendix.

Most of the new approaches introduced in this monograph can be estimated using OnFront3, see www.emq.com.

Chapter 1

ESSAY 1: EFFICIENCY INDICATORS AND INDEXES

This essay focuses on two approaches to measuring efficiency, namely the difference approach and the ratio approach. In the index number theory literature, Diewert (1998) classifies measures that are in difference form as **indicators** and measures that take the form of ratios as **indexes**, a terminology which we shall adopt here. As Diewert points out, the ratio approach is the 'traditional (bilateral) approach to index number theory.' Examples include the cost of living index (ratios of cost functions) as well as the familiar Paasche and Laspeyres price and quantity indexes. Diewert also points out that the difference approach pioneered by Bennet (1920) and Montgomery (1929, 1937) was largely forgotten, except for the difference quantity indicator, most familiar as a measure of consumer surplus.

A unifying feature of our approach to efficiency measurement is that whether difference or ratio based, they are all rooted in duality theory, which is also the basis by which we decompose our efficiency measures. The 'value' or dual measures are support functions such as profit, cost and revenue functions. Primal measures are their dual distance functions. This approach to efficiency measurement yields a natural correspondence between quantity and value measures. As we shall see below, the profit function with its additive structure finds its perfect match with the directional distance function which shares that structure. The more familiar cost and revenue-based Farrell efficiency indexes are multiplicative as are the Shephard type distance functions which are their duals. Eventually we shall see that the revenue and cost indexes and their duals are in fact special cases of the profit and directional distance function, providing an elegant overarching structure.

This essay opens with the 'forgotten' indicator approach; we begin with a profit indicator and its decomposition. This section introduces the key technical efficiency component used in the indicator approach, namely the **Directional Distance Function**. This is followed with the parallel indicators for revenue and cost which also use special cases of the directional distance function. Next we turn to the ratio forms of efficiency indexes, including revenue and cost efficiency and their decompositions. The next section 'From Indicators to Indexes' links the two approaches; the final section shows how the ratio approach can be related to profits by employing the special case of hyperbolic efficiency and the modified profit concept of return to the dollar.

1. The Nerlovian Profit Indicator

Perhaps the most natural measure of performance that is based on differences is profit; so it follows that the natural form for a measure of **profit efficiency** is as a difference rather than as a ratio. This is also practical, since firms may earn zero profit, which poses problems in a ratio context. Thus we begin this essay by developing an indicator of profit efficiency which we dub the Nerlovian profit indicator along with technical and allocative component indicators.

As noted above, construction of a measure of profit efficiency based on ratios is impractical due to the fact that both maximal and observed profit may equal zero. The ratio of maximal to observed profit may be infinite, which is not meaningful. To avoid these problems, the Nerlovian profit indicator is defined as the difference between price deflated maximal profit and price deflated observed profit. The additive structure of the profit indicator carries over to its components; i.e., their sum equals the profit indicator.

We begin with some notation. Input quantities are denoted by

$$x = (x_1, \ldots, x_N) \in \Re^N_+$$

and their associated prices by

$$w = (w_1, \ldots, w_N) \in \Re^N_+.$$

The circumstance that inputs and their prices are real numbers implies that they are fully divisible. Inputs may be applied in any fraction and any real number may be quoted or chosen as a price.

Cost is the inner product of inputs and their prices, and is denoted by

$$wx = \sum_{n=1}^{N} w_n x_n. \tag{1.1}$$

Assuming that output quantities and their prices are divisible we may denote output quantities by

$$y = (y_1, \ldots, y_M) \in \Re_+^M$$

with associated prices

$$p = (p_1, \ldots, p_M) \in \Re_+^M.$$

Their inner product defines **Revenue**,

$$py = \sum_{m=1}^{M} p_m y_m, \tag{1.2}$$

and the difference between revenue and cost yields **Profit**

$$py - wx = \sum_{m=1}^{M} p_m y_m - \sum_{n=1}^{N} w_n x_n. \tag{1.3}$$

Our profit efficiency indicator measures the difference between maximum and observed profit. To define maximum profit we need to introduce a set from which the 'optimal' input output bundle (x^*, y^*) can be chosen. The natural set for this purpose is the **Technology** defined as

$$T = \{(x, y) : x \text{ can produce } y\}. \tag{1.4}$$

In the appendix at the end of the manuscript we introduce axioms that the technology should satisfy, but for the moment we may think of T simply as a nonempty, closed set.

Now we may define maximum profit as

$$\Pi(p, w) = \sup\{py - wx : (x, y) \in T\}. \tag{1.5}$$

We illustrate the underlying optimization problem in Figure 1.1.

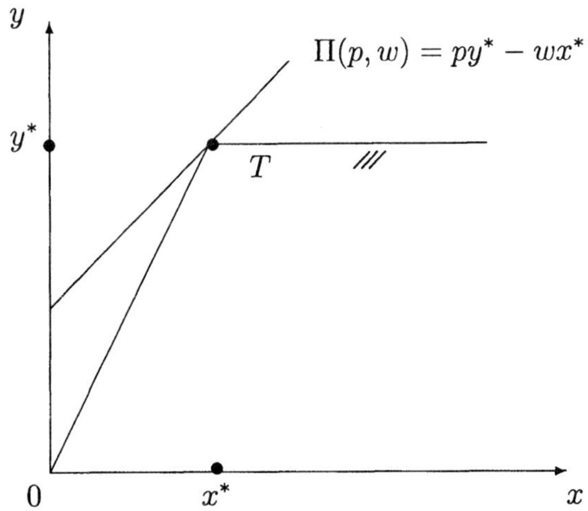

Figure 1.1. Profit Maximization

In the figure, the technology is bounded by the broken line emanating from the origin. The slope of the hyperplane which touches the technology at the kink is determined by the input and output prices. Thus the solution to the profit maximization problem is the input output vector (x^*, y^*), with associated maximum profit:

$$\Pi(p, w) = py^* - wx^*. \tag{1.6}$$

The function $\Pi(p, w)$ is called the **Profit Function**, and when it exists it satisfies the following conditions:

Π.1 nonnegative, nonincreasing in w and nondecreasing in p

Π.2 homogeneous of degree +1 in (w, p)

Π.3 convex and continuous in positive prices.[1]

[1]The proof of these conditions can be found in standard textbooks such as Varian (1992).

Given the maximal profit $\Pi(p,w)$, let $\Pi^k = py^k - wx^k$ denote firm $k's$ observed profit, then the **Nerlovian Profit Indicator** is defined as

$$NI(p,w,y^k,x^k;g_x,g_y) = \frac{\Pi(p,w)-\Pi^k}{pg_y+wg_x} = \frac{p(y^*-y^k)-w(x^*-x^k)}{pg_y+wg_x}. \tag{1.7}$$

The vectors $g_x \in \Re_+^N$ and $g_y \in \Re_+^M$ are the **Directional Vectors** in which efficiency is evaluated. These will be discussed in more detail when we introduce directional distance functions.

The Nerlovian profit indicator is defined as a difference which implies that zero profit poses no computational problems. This indicator also has the desirable property of being homogeneous of degree zero in prices—so its value won't change if we switch from lira to dollars for example. We say that firm k is **Profit Efficient** if $NI(p,w,y^k,x^k;g_x,g_y) = 0$, i.e., if and only if

$$py^* - wx^* = \Pi(p,w) = \Pi^k = py^k - wx^k.$$

Put differently, firm k is profit efficient if it achieves maximum profit.

Since $\Pi(p,w)$ is by definition greater than or equal to observed profit Π^k, it follows that our profit indicator is greater than or equal to zero, with profit inefficiency signaled when the indicator is greater than zero.

At this point, we would like to characterize the input output vector associated with Nerlovian profit efficiency. We begin by introducing

Definition (1):
The input output vector $(x,y) \in T$ is **Technology Efficient** if there does not exist another $(x^{'},y^{'}) \in T$ such that $(-x^{'},y^{'}) \geqq (-x,y)$, $(x^{'},y^{'}) \neq (x,y)$. The set of technology efficient input output vectors is denoted by $EffT$.

This leads to the following

Proposition (1):
If (x,y) maximizes profit for strictly positive prices $p_m > 0, m = 1,\ldots,M$ and $w_n > 0, n = 1,\ldots,N$ then (x,y) is technology efficient, i.e., $(x,y) \in EffT$.

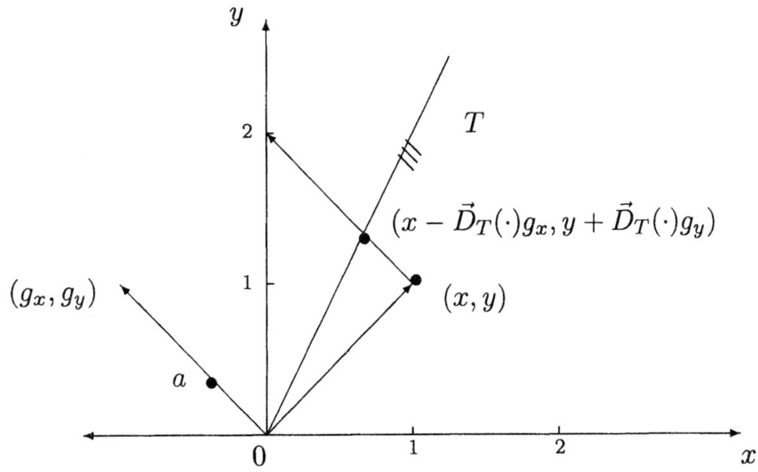

Figure 1.2. Directional Technology Distance Function

This proposition tells us that if a firm k is profit efficient and prices are strictly positive, then its input output choice (x^k, y^k) is efficient. See the Appendix for the proof.

Next we decompose the Nerlovian profit indicator into a technical and an allocative component. We will define the allocative component as a residual, thus we turn our attention first to technical efficiency. Here we will measure technical efficiency with a directional distance function. This distance function differs from the traditional Shephard type distance functions in several ways. For example, as its name implies the directional distance function is associated with an explicit direction in which efficiency is gauged. This requires that we specify a direction vector (g_x, g_y), which we use to define

$$\vec{D}_T(x, y; g_x, g_y) = \sup\{\beta : (x - \beta g_x, y + \beta g_y) \in T\}. \qquad (1.8)$$

The function above is called the **Directional Technology Distance Function.** It 'expands' outputs in the direction g_y and 'contracts' inputs in the direction g_x. Figure 1.2 illustrates.

The technology T consists of the area between and including the x-axis and the ray emanating from the origin. The directional vector $g = (g_x, g_y)$ is located in the 4:th quadrant, indicating that output is expanded and input is contracted. The distance function translates the

(x, y) vector in the direction (g_x, g_y) onto the boundary of the technology. Since (x, y) is interior to technology T, the value of the distance function is greater than zero; here it is equal to $0a/0g$, where $0g$ is the ray from the origin to (g_x, g_y).

In order to provide some intuition, we turn to an explicit example of a directional distance function. Let's assume that the technology takes the simple form of

$$T = \{(x, y) : y \leqq 2x, x \geqq 0\}.$$

If we choose $x = 1, y = 1$ we obviously have an inefficient bundle, since our technology could produce two units of output with 1 unit of input. If we choose $g_x = 1, g_y = 1$, then substituting into the definition of the directional distance function we have

$$\vec{D}_T(1, 1; 1, 1) = \sup\{\beta : (1 - \beta, 1 + \beta) \in T\}.$$

The solution is found by solving the following inequality

$$y + \beta \leqq 2(x - \beta), \text{ for } y = 1, x = 1.$$

In this case we have $\beta^* = \vec{D}_T(1, 1; 1, 1) = 1/3$, with $x^* = 1 - 1/3 = 2/3$ and $y^* = 1 + 1/3 = 4/3$.

To establish a relationship between profit efficiency and the directional distance function we must first prove that the translated vector is feasible, i.e., that

$$(x - \vec{D}_T(x, y; g_x, g_y)g_x, y + \vec{D}_T(x, y; g_x, g_y)g_y) \in T. \tag{1.9}$$

This condition is satisfied provided that the technology T is a closed set and satisfies free disposability of inputs and outputs (see the Axioms of Production Appendix), since then there exists a scalar β such that $(x - \beta g_x, y + \beta g_y)$ is feasible, i.e., it belongs to the technology.

Armed with this feasibility condition we are ready to develop the (dual) relation between profit efficiency and the directional distance function. From the definition of maximum profit (1.5), we have

$$\Pi(p, w) \geqq py - wx \text{ for all } (x, y) \in T. \tag{1.10}$$

Thus by the feasibility condition,

$$\begin{aligned}\Pi(p,w) &\geqq p(y+\vec{D}_T(x,y;g_x,g_y)g_y) \\ &\quad -w(x-\vec{D}_T(x,y;g_x,g_y)g_x) \\ &= (py-wx)+\vec{D}_T(x,y;g_x,g_y)(pg_y+wg_x),\end{aligned} \tag{1.11}$$

or

$$\frac{\Pi(p,w)-(py-wx)}{pg_y+wg_x} \geqq \vec{D}_T(x,y;g_x,g_y). \tag{1.12}$$

On the left hand side of the inequality we have the Nerlovian profit indicator and on the right hand side is the directional distance function. Thus we have a price (dual) and a quantity (primal) measure of efficiency. In general they need not coincide, thus there can be a residual or a duality gap. We call this gap allocative efficiency, and it allows us to decompose the profit indicator into two parts: technical and allocative efficiency,

$$\frac{\Pi(p,w)-(py-wx)}{pg_y+wg_x} = \vec{D}_T(x,y;g_x,g_y)+\vec{AE}_T. \tag{1.13}$$

Our decomposition differs from the standard Farrell multiplicative decomposition in that it is additive, namely the overall (profit) efficiency is the sum of the two efficiency components.

As an efficiency measure we are interested in the properties of the directional distance function. From the definition, we obtain the following **Translation Property**

$\vec{\mathbf{D}}_\mathbf{T}.1$ $\vec{D}_T(x-\alpha g_x, y+\alpha g_y; g_x, g_y) = \vec{D}_T(x,y;g_x,g_y)-\alpha, \alpha \in \Re.$

This condition tells us that if we translate the input output vector (x,y) into $(x-\alpha g_x, y+\alpha g_y)$, then the value of the distance function is reduced by the scalar α. This translation property is the 'additive' analog of the 'multiplicative' homogeneity property of the usual Shephard distance functions.

A second property is that the directional distance function is **Homogeneous of Degree -1** in the directional vector (g_x, g_y), i.e.,

$\vec{\mathbf{D}}_\mathbf{T}.2$ $\vec{D}_T(x,y;\lambda g_x,\lambda g_y) = \lambda^{-1}\vec{D}_T(x,y;g_x,g_y), \lambda > 0.$

If inputs and outputs are freely or strongly disposable (see the production axioms appendix) then the distance function has the **Representation Property**:

$\vec{\mathbf{D}}_{\mathbf{T}}$.3 $\vec{D}_T(x, y; g_x, g_y) \geqq 0$ if and only if $(x, y) \in T$.

In words, the distance function completely characterizes the technology. Hence the conditions imposed on the underlying technology T have analogs in terms of the properties of the distance function.

If inputs are freely disposable then the distance function is nondecreasing in x and if outputs are freely disposable then it is nonincreasing in y, i.e.,

$\vec{\mathbf{D}}_{\mathbf{T}}$.4 $x' \geqq x$ implies $\vec{D}_T(x', y; g_x, g_y) \geqq \vec{D}_T(x, y; g_x, g_y)$.

$\vec{\mathbf{D}}_{\mathbf{T}}$.5 $y' \geqq y$ implies $\vec{D}_T(x, y'; g_x, g_y) \leqq \vec{D}_T(x, y; g_x, g_y)$.

If the technology exhibits **Constant Returns to Scale** i.e., $\lambda T = T, \lambda > 0$, then we have

$\vec{\mathbf{D}}_{\mathbf{T}}$.6 $\vec{D}_T(\lambda x, \lambda y; g_x, g_y) = \lambda \vec{D}_T(x, y; g_x, g_y), \lambda > 0$.

In this case the distance function is homogeneous of degree +1 in inputs and outputs.

Having established some of the properties of our measure of technical efficiency, we now can say that a firm is **Efficient in the** (g_x, g_y) **direction** or (g_x, g_y)**-Efficient** if

$$\vec{D}_T(x, y; g_x, g_y) = 0. \tag{1.14}$$

Clearly, efficiency depends on the choice of the directional vector as we illustrate in Figure 1.3.

The technology is labeled T and our input output vector (x, y) belongs to the boundary of the technology. If we choose $(-1, 1)$ as the directional vector, then (x, y) is efficient. If however, we choose $(-1, 0)$ instead, then it is not efficient.

As the reader has likely noticed, directional efficiency as defined in (1.14) is a different notion than the efficiency notion introduced earlier in terms of inequalities. Their relation is illustrated by the following

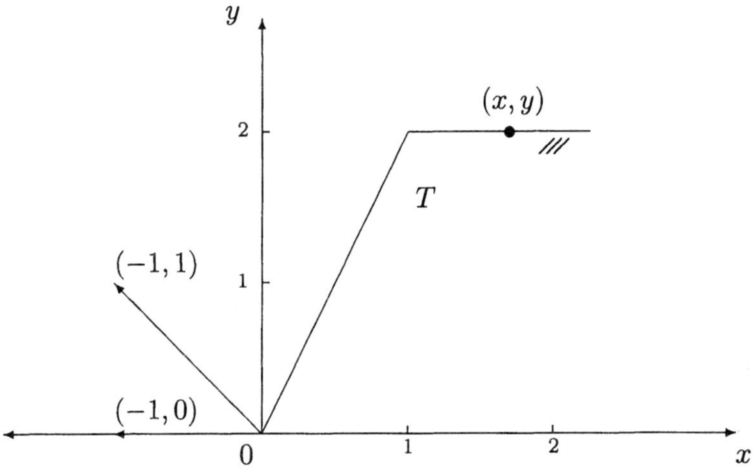

Figure 1.3. Efficiency and Direction Vectors

proposition. See Appendix for proof.

Proposition (2):
If a feasible vector $(x, y) \notin EffT$ then there exists a directional vector (g_x, g_y) such that $\vec{D}_T(x, y; g_x, g_y) > 0$. If $(x, y) \in EffT$ then $\vec{D}_T(x, y; g_x, g_y) = 0$ for all $(g_x, g_y) \neq 0$.

This proposition shows that there exist directional vectors such that the distance function can identify inefficiency as defined earlier. However, we do not have a general rule for determining those vectors.

Next we show how the Nerlovian profit indicator and its component indicators may be estimated based on linear programming problems. Suppose that we have $k = 1, \ldots, K$ observations of inputs and outputs. From these we can construct a reference technology T, satisfying variable returns to scale as

$$T = \{(x, y) : \sum_{k=1}^{K} z_k y_{km} \geqq y_m, m = 1, \ldots, M, \tag{1.15}$$

$$\sum_{k=1}^{K} z_k x_{kn} \leqq x_n, n = 1, \ldots, N,$$

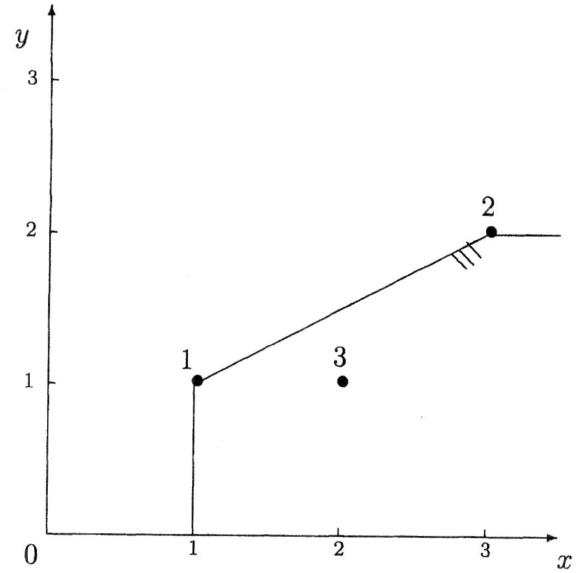

Figure 1.4. A Technology

$$\sum_{k=1}^{K} z_k = 1, z_k \geqq 0, k = 1, \ldots, K\}.$$

We illustrate the construction of this reference technology with the following data set.

Obs. k	Input x	Output y
1	1	1
2	3	2
3	2	1

Table 1.1 Data

The three observations $k = 1, 2, 3$ are denoted by dots in Figure 1.4. The line segment connecting 1 and 2 is constructed by varying the intensity variables z_1 and z_2. The area 'under' the line is included in the technology due to free disposability of inputs and outputs, which is reflected in the inequalities in the input and output constraints.

Using the data from Table 1.1, the technology may be written as

$$\begin{aligned} T = \{(x, y) : & \; z_1 1 + z_2 2 + z_3 1 \geqq y, \\ & \; z_1 1 + z_2 3 + z_3 2 \leqq x, \\ & \; z_1 + z_2 + z_3 = 1, \\ & \; z_1 \geqq 0, z_2 \geqq 0, z_3 \geqq 0\}, \end{aligned} \tag{1.16}$$

In (1.15) and subsequently in (1.16) we have restricted the intensity variables $z_k, k = 1, \ldots, K$ to sum to one. This allows for the possibility of negative, positive or zero profit.

Given input and output prices (w, p), maximum profit can be estimated by solving the linear programming problem

$$\begin{aligned} \Pi(p, w) &= \max_{x,y} \sum_{m=1}^{M} p_m y_m - \sum_{n=1}^{N} w_n x_n \\ & s.t. \sum_{k=1}^{K} z_k y_{km} \geqq y_m, m = 1, \ldots, M, \\ & \sum_{k=1}^{K} z_k x_{kn} \leqq x_n, n = 1, \ldots, N, \\ & \sum_{k=1}^{K} z_k = 1, z_k \geqq 0, k = 1, \ldots, K. \end{aligned} \tag{1.17}$$

If different observations face different prices, the explicit prices would then be substituted into the objective function and the solution would be denoted by $\Pi(p^k, w^k)$. In our example if all of our observations face output price $p = 1$ and input price $w = 1$, then maximum profit would be achieved with $(x^*, y^*) = (1, 1)$ and maximum profit $\Pi(p, w) = 0$.

The solution to (1.17) together with an explicit choice of a directional vector suffice to estimate the overall Nerlovian profit indicator in (1.7). To estimate the technical efficiency component one may solve a linear programming problem for each observation $k' = 1, \ldots, K$

$$\begin{aligned} \vec{D}_T(x^{k'}, y^{k'}; g_x, g_y) &= \max \beta \\ & s.t. \sum_{k=1}^{K} z_k y_{km} \geqq y_{k'm} + \beta g_{y_m}, m = 1, \ldots, M, \end{aligned} \tag{1.18}$$

$$\sum_{k=1}^{K} z_k x_{kn} \leqq x_{k'n} - \beta g_{x_n}, n = 1, \ldots, N,$$
$$\sum_{k=1}^{K} z_k = 1, z_k \geqq 0, k = 1, \ldots, K.$$

In our example above, if we chose the direction vector $(g_x, g_y) = (1,1)$, then both observation 1 and 2 would be technically efficient with $\vec{D}_T(x, y; g_x, g_y) = 0$, whereas observation 3 is technically inefficient with $\vec{D}_T(x, y; g_x, g_y) > 0$.

As noted earlier, allocative efficiency $\vec{AE}_T$ is a residual and may be computed as the difference between profit efficiency and technical efficiency. To be explicit, assume that we have estimated maximum profit for an observation k facing prices (p^k, w^k), i.e., we have $\Pi(p^k, w^k)$. Then the Nerlovian profit indicator is

$$NI(p^k, w^k, y^k, x^k; g_x, g_y) = \frac{\Pi(p^k, w^k) - (p^k y^k - w^k x^k)}{p^k g_y + w^k g_x}.$$

Also assume that we have estimated the directional distance function

$$\vec{D}_T(x^k, y^k; g_x, g_y),$$

then the allocative efficiency component is obtained as a difference,

$$\vec{AE}_T^k = NI(p^k, w^k, y^k, x^k; g_x, g_y) - \vec{D}_T(x^k, y^k; g_x, g_y).$$

For our numerical example, observation 1 is the only profit efficient firm; observation 3 deviates from profit efficiency due both to technical and allocative inefficiency, whereas firm 2 is only allocatively inefficient. An extended empirical application is provided in Essay 3.

2. The Revenue Efficiency Indicator

We now turn to the revenue indicator which we define as the difference between maximal and observed revenue, normalized by the value of the output directional vector (pg_y). This is in contrast to the traditional Farrell revenue efficiency which is defined as a ratio as we shall see when we discuss it later in this essay. There we also provide a link between the additive indicator approach and the ratio index approach to revenue efficiency.

Maximal revenue is defined in terms of the **Output Sets** $P(x)$

$$P(x) = \{y : (x, y) \in T\}, x \in \Re_+^N, \tag{1.19}$$

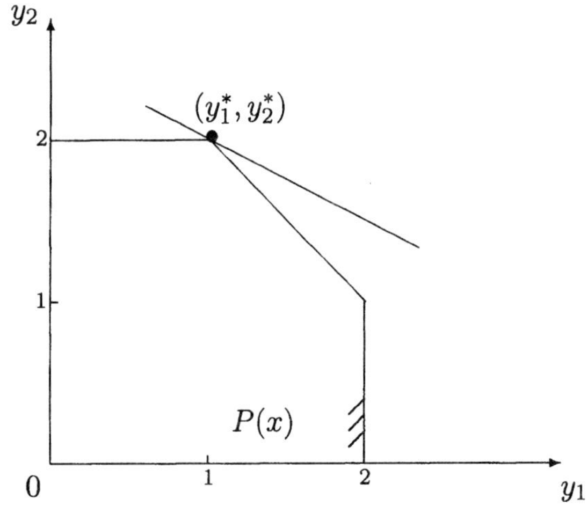

Figure 1.5. Revenue Maximization

as

$$R(x,p) = \max\{py : y \in P(x)\}. \tag{1.20}$$

The function $R(x,p)$ is called the **Revenue Function** and if we assume that $P(x)$ is a nonempty, compact set (see the production axioms), the maximum is achieved. If output prices are positive, the revenue function satisfies the following properties:

R.1 $R(x,p)$ is nonnegative and nondecreasing in output prices

R.2 $R(x,p)$ is homogeneous of degree one in output prices

R.3 $R(x,p)$ is continuous and convex in output prices.

We include an illustration of the definition of the revenue function in Figure 1.5.

The technology is characterized by its output set $P(x)$ and it consists of the area between and including the broken line and the two y-axes. The revenue maximization problem yields (y_1^*, y_2^*) as its solution and the resulting maximal revenue equals

$$R(x,p) = \sum_{m=1}^{M} p_m y_m^* = py^*. \tag{1.21}$$

In our essay on environmental performance, we allow for the possibility that some outputs may be undesirable. There we also allow the prices of undesirable outputs to be nonpositive. This will not alter $R.2$ and $R.3$ above, but property $R.1$ must be adjusted to reflect the condition that some prices may be negative.

If we denote observed revenue by $R^k = py^k$, then the **Revenue Efficiency Indicator** is defined as

$$RI(x^k, y^k, p; g_y) = \frac{R(x^k, p) - R^k}{pg_y} = \frac{p(y^* - y^k)}{pg_y} \tag{1.22}$$

The vector $g_y \in \Re^M_+, g_y \neq 0$ is the directional output vector. Thus we are normalizing the revenue difference by the value of the directional vector, which has the effect of making the indicator independent of the units in which prices are measured.

As we show below, the revenue efficiency indicator may be derived as a special case of the Nerlovian profit indicator. To see this, take $g_x = 0$ and assume that observed cost wx^k is equal to minimum cost wx^*, then

$$\begin{aligned} NI(p^k, w^k, y^k, x^k; g_x, g_y) &= \frac{R(x^k, p) - wx^*}{pg_y} \\ &\quad - \frac{(py^k - wx^k)}{pg_y} \\ &= \frac{R(x^k, p) - py^k}{pg_y} \\ &= RI(x^k, y^k, p; g_y). \end{aligned} \tag{1.23}$$

We say that an observation is **Revenue Efficient** if $RI(x, y, p; g_y) = 0$, which occurs when the firm maximizes revenue. In our discussion of profit efficiency we isolated the efficient subset of the technology T, $EffT$ which denoted the efficient input output vectors. Here we need only identify efficient output vectors; since maximum revenue identifies efficient outputs (and not inputs) we focus on outputs alone. We define the set of **Efficient Output Vectors** as

$$EffP(x) = \{y : y \in P(x), y' \geqq y, y' \neq y, \text{ then } y' \notin P(x)\}, \tag{1.24}$$

then if output prices are positive, $p_m > 0, m = 1, \ldots, M$, revenue efficiency implies that the observed output vector y^k is an efficient output vector. The formal proof that if prices are positive then the optimizer belongs to the efficient output set is left to the reader. The proof is similar to showing that a profit maximizing input output vector belongs to the efficient technology set.

The revenue indicator may also be decomposed into technical and allocative components. The technical efficiency component is called the **Directional Output Distance Function** and it is defined as

$$\vec{D}_o(x, y; g_y) = \sup\{\beta : (y + \beta g_y) \in P(x)\}. \tag{1.25}$$

Clearly this can be derived from $\vec{D}_T(x, y; g_x, g_y)$ by setting $g_x = 0$, thus

$$\vec{D}_o(x, y; g_y) = \vec{D}_T(x, y; 0, g_y). \tag{1.26}$$

Formally, if $(x, y) \in T$ then $(x, y + \beta g_y) \in T$ which is equivalent to $(y + \beta g_y) \in P(x)$. From this observation and its definition it is easy to deduce the following properties of the directional output distance function:

$\vec{\mathbf{D}}_\mathbf{o}$.1 $\vec{D}_o(x, y + \alpha g_y; g_y) = \vec{D}_o(x, y; g_y) - \alpha, \alpha \in \Re$, **(Translation)**.

$\vec{\mathbf{D}}_\mathbf{o}$.2 $\vec{D}_o(x, y; \lambda g_y) = \lambda^{-1}\vec{D}_o(x, y; g_y), \lambda > 0$, **(Homogeneity of degree -1 in the directional vector)**.

$\vec{\mathbf{D}}_\mathbf{o}$.3 If outputs are strongly disposable, then $\vec{D}_o(x, y; g_y) \geqq 0$ if and only if $y \in P(x)$, **(Representation)**.

$\vec{\mathbf{D}}_\mathbf{o}$.4 If inputs are strongly disposable, then $\vec{D}_o(x, y; g_y)$ is nondecreasing in inputs.

$\vec{\mathbf{D}}_\mathbf{o}$.5 If outputs are strongly disposable, then $\vec{D}_o(x, y; g_y)$ is nonincreasing in outputs.

$\vec{\mathbf{D}}_\mathbf{o}$.6 If the technology exhibits constant returns to scale, i.e., $P(\theta x) = \theta P(x), \theta > 0$, then $\vec{D}_o(\theta x, \theta y; g_y) = \theta \vec{D}_o(x, y; g_y), \theta > 0$.

We include an illustration of the directional output distance function in Figure 1.6.

The technology is represented by the output set $P(x)$. The direction vector $g_y = (g_{y_1}, g_{y_2})$ is positive since both outputs (y_1, y_2) are assumed to be desirable. The distance function expands the outputs in the direction g_y until the boundary is attained.

In the special case of a single output, the directional output distance function takes the form

$$\vec{D}_o(x, y; 1) = F(x) - y,$$

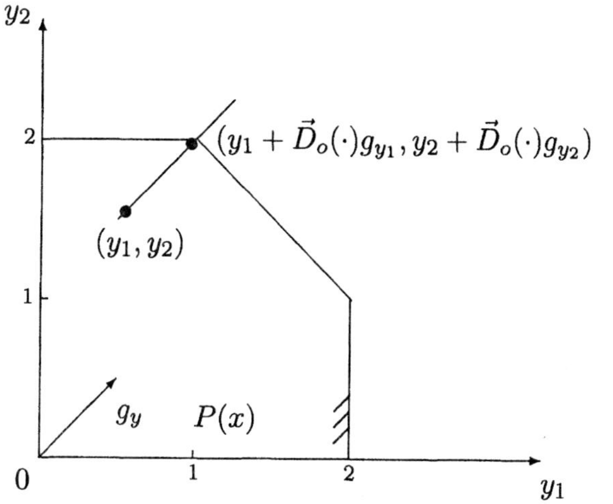

Figure 1.6. The Directional Output Distance Function

where $F(x) = \max\{y : y \in P(x)\}$ is a **Production Function**. By the translation property we also have the following result for this case

$$\vec{D}_o(x, y; 1) = \vec{D}_o(x, 0; 1) - y.$$

Thus we may interpret $\vec{D}_o(x, 0; 1)$ as a production function. To see this we just equate the last two expressions for $\vec{D}_o(x, y; 1)$.

To connect the directional output distance function to our notion of technical efficiency, we say that an observation is **Efficient in the g_y direction** or **g_y-Efficient** if

$$\vec{D}_o(x, y; g_y) = 0. \tag{1.27}$$

Again, the efficiency of an observation depends on the choice of direction which we illustrate in Figure 1.7.

Consider two directions $(1, 1)$ and $(1, 0)$. In the first case the output vector (y_1, y_2) is g_y-efficient, but in the second case it is not.

The relationship between output and g_y-efficiency is summarized in the following proposition.

Proposition (3):
If $y \notin EffP(x)$ then there exists a directional vector $g_y \neq 0$ such

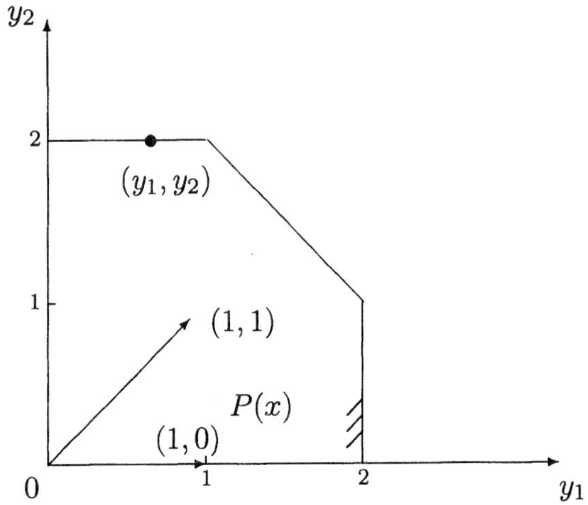

Figure 1.7. g_y-Efficiency

that $\vec{D}_o(x, y; g_y) > 0$. If $y \in EffP(x)$ then $\vec{D}_o(x, y; g_y) = 0$ for all $g_y \neq 0, g_y \in \Re^M_+$.

Figure 1.7 also illustrates the fact that the boundary of $P(x)$ between the y_1 and y_2 axes is not necessarily equivalent to $EffP(x)$. In our case, the boundary of $P(x)$ between the y_1 and y_2 axes is the **Output Isoquant** which we define as

$$IsoqP(x) = \{y : y \in P(x), \theta y \notin P(x), \theta > 1\}, x \in \Re^N_+. \quad (1.28)$$

This subset of the output set is defined by radially expanding the feasible output vectors. This should be contrasted with the definition of the efficient subset $EffP(x)$, in which inequalities are used. We note that in general we have

$$EffP(x) \subseteq IsoqP(x). \quad (1.29)$$

Again, Figure 1.7 illustrates the case in which the efficient subset is a proper subset of the isoquant. The isoquant is the outer boundary of the set between (y_1, y_2)=(0,2) and (y_1, y_2)=(2,0), while the efficient subset is the downward sloping middle segment of the outer boundary.

We are now able to explicitly characterize the relation between g_y-efficiency and the isoquant. This is done by the two following propositions:

Proposition (4):
Let g_y be strictly positive, i.e., $g_{y_m} > 0, m = 1, \ldots, M$. If $y \in IsoqP(x)$, then $\vec{D}_o(x, y; g_y) = 0$.

Proposition (5):
Let y and g_y be strictly positive, i.e., $y_m > 0, g_{y_m} > 0, m = 1, \ldots, M$, and let outputs be freely disposable. If $\vec{D}_o(x, y; g_y) = 0$, then $y \in IsoqP(x)$.

The first of the two propositions tells us that if an output vector belongs to the output isoquant, then the directional distance function takes the value of zero when evaluated in any strictly positive direction. The second proposition is a partial converse to the first. The 'partialness' is due to the fact that outputs must be strictly positive in the second proposition, but not in the first.

Next we derive the decomposition of revenue efficiency into technical and allocative components. From the revenue maximization problem (1.20) we know that

$$R(x, p) \geqq py \text{ for all } y \in P(x). \tag{1.30}$$

and since $(y + \vec{D}_o(x, y; g_y)g_y) \in P(x)$, we have

$$\frac{R(x, p) - py}{pg_y} \geqq \vec{D}_o(x, y; g_y). \tag{1.31}$$

The left hand side of this expression is our revenue efficiency indicator, and the right hand side is the associated measure of technical efficiency. This relationship may also be derived directly from our profit efficiency indicator, see Section 1.5.

Since revenue efficiency in general does not equal technical efficiency, we add a residual term to close the gap, namely allocative efficiency $\vec{AE}_o$.

$$RI(x, y, p; g_y) = \frac{R(x, p) - py}{pg_y} = \vec{D}_o(x, y; g_y) + \vec{AE}_o. \tag{1.32}$$

This decomposition of the revenue efficiency indicator into technical and allocative efficiency is illustrated in Figure 1.8.

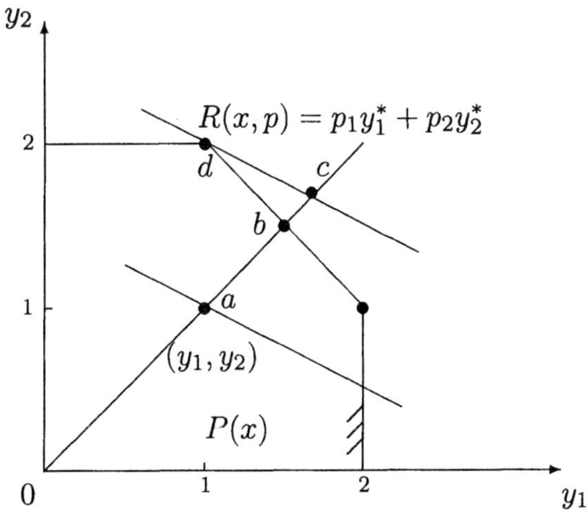

Figure 1.8. Decomposition of the Revenue Indicator

The overall revenue efficiency indicator gives a normalized value of the difference between maximum revenue $R(x,p)$ and observed revenue $p_1y_1 + p_2y_2$. Observed revenue is denoted by point a and maximum revenue $R(x,p)$ is determined by the revenue hyperplane going through c and just touching the boundary of $P(x)$ at d. In order to isolate technical efficiency, we must choose a direction vector; here we have chosen the direction $(1,1)$, which expands the output vector (y_1, y_2) from a to the boundary at b. The residual between b and c is the allocative efficiency component.

In terms of empirical implementation, we can estimate the revenue indicator and its components as solutions to simple linear programming problems, as we did for the profit indicator. Again, assume that we have $k = 1, \ldots, K$ observations of inputs and outputs, (x^k, y^k). From these we can construct the output sets for each k' as

$$\begin{aligned} P(x^{k'}) &= \{y : \sum_{k=1}^{K} z_k y_{km} \geqq y_m, m = 1, \ldots, M, \\ &\qquad \sum_{k=1}^{K} z_k x_{kn} \leqq x_{k'n}, n = 1, \ldots, N, \\ &\qquad z_k \geqq 0, k = 1, \ldots, K\}. \end{aligned} \tag{1.33}$$

This technology has strongly disposable inputs and outputs and in contrast to our assumption on T for the profit efficiency indicator, for convenience we impose constant returns to scale rather than variable returns to scale (see the production axioms). This follows from the fact that we have omitted the $\sum_{k=1}^{K} z_k = 1$ constraint, which allowed for zero maximal profit as well as losses. One could, however, impose variable returns to scale here as well. If in addition, output prices are known, we may solve for maximum revenue for each observation $k' = 1, \ldots, K$ as the solution to the following problem.

$$\begin{aligned} R(x^{k'}, p) \quad &= \quad \max \sum_{m=1}^{M} p_m y_m \\ s.t. \quad &\sum_{k=1}^{K} z_k y_{km} \geqq y_m, m = 1, \ldots, M, \\ &\sum_{k=1}^{K} z_k x_{kn} \leqq x_{k'n}, n = 1, \ldots, N, \\ &z_k \geqq 0, k = 1, \ldots, K. \end{aligned} \tag{1.34}$$

Together with observed revenue $py^{k'}$ and a choice of the directional vector g_y, we can estimate the revenue efficiency indicator in (1.32). To estimate technical efficiency requires solving the following linear programming problem for each observation $k' = 1, \ldots, K$

$$\begin{aligned} \vec{D}_o(x^{k'}, y^{k'}; g_y) \quad &= \quad \max \beta \\ s.t. \quad &\sum_{k=1}^{K} z_k y_{km} \geqq y_{k'm} + \beta g_{ym}, m = 1, \ldots, M, \\ &\sum_{k=1}^{K} z_k x_{kn} \leqq x_{k'n}, n = 1, \ldots, N, \\ &z_k \geqq 0, k = 1, \ldots, K. \end{aligned} \tag{1.35}$$

One empirical detail is the choice of the direction vector g_y. Some practical choices include the unit vector, which implies that all observations will be evaluated in the same direction. This choice has the additional benefit of facilitating aggregation, see Essay 3. Another obvious choice would be to choose the observed output vector as the direction of evaluation. This has the advantage of familiarity—this is the direction of a Farrell output oriented technical efficiency measure. This also allows us to interpret the solution as a percent potential increase in output.

As usual, allocative efficiency $\vec{AE}_o$ is obtained as a residual.

The linear programming problem above imposes i) strong disposability of outputs, ii) strong disposability of inputs and iii) constant returns to scale. Each of these three assumptions may be relaxed to fit specific model requirements. Moreover, in Essay 2 we show how the directional distance function may be estimated parametrically.

3. Cost Efficiency Indicator

Although the development of a cost efficiency indicator mirrors that of the profit and revenue indicators developed in the previous sections, we include the details here for readers who have not read those earlier sections.

Again, beginning with basic notational conventions, we denote observed cost as

$$wx = \sum_{n=1}^{N} w_n x_n,$$

where $w_n \geqq 0, n = 1, \ldots, N$ are input prices and the corresponding x_n are input quantities. Moreover, let $C(y, w)$ be the cost function (defined below) and let x^* be the optimal input vector such that

$$C(y, w) = wx^*.$$

Finally we let $g_x \in \Re_+^N$ denote a directional input vector. We are now ready to define our **Cost Efficiency Indicator** as

$$CI(x, y, w; g_x) = \frac{wx - C(y, w)}{wg_x} = \frac{w(x - x^*)}{wg_x}. \tag{1.36}$$

Since $C(y, w) \leqq wx$ for all feasible input vectors (see the definition below), the indicator is nonnegative. It signals efficiency if the value is zero. This indicator can be derived from the Nerlovian profit indicator by taking $g_y = 0$ and assuming that observed revenue py is equal to maximum revenue.

Turning to the cost function, we first define the **Input Requirement Sets**

$$L(y) = \{x : (x, y) \in T\}, y \in \Re_+^M. \tag{1.37}$$

The cost function is then defined as

$$C(y,w) = \min\{wx : x \in L(y)\}. \tag{1.38}$$

If prices are strictly positive, i.e., $w_n > 0, n = 1, \ldots, N$, and $L(y)$ is a nonempty closed set (see the production axioms), then the **Cost Function** $C(y,w)$ is well-defined, i.e., the minimum exists and it satisfies the following properties:

C.1 $C(y,w)$ is nonnegative and nondecreasing in input prices.

C.2 $C(y,w)$ is homogeneous of degree one in input prices.

C.3 $C(y,w)$ is continuous and concave in (positive) input prices.

We illustrate the cost minimization problem in Figure 1.9.

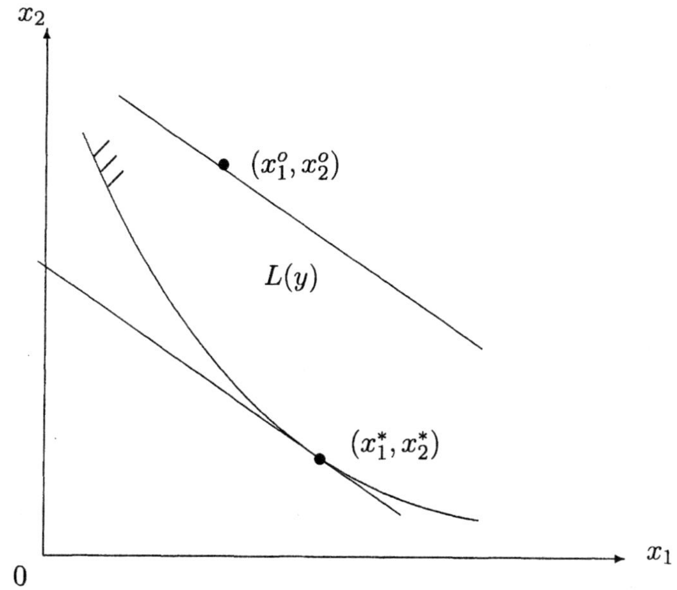

Figure 1.9. Cost Minimization

The input requirement set $L(y)$ is the area above and including the curved line. At positive prices, the minimum cost is achieved with the input vector (x_1^*, x_2^*). Whenever the input requirement set is expressed as an activity analysis model, then the efficient input set is bounded, which means that we need not assume that prices are strictly positive to define the cost function.

We say that an observation is **Cost Efficient** if $CI(x, y, w; g_x) = 0$, which occurs when the firm minimizes cost, as in Figure 1.9 at (x_1^*, x_2^*). To interpret cost efficiency in terms of the input requirement set, we define the **Efficient Input Set** as

$$EffL(y) = \{x : x \in L(y), x' \leqq x, x' \neq x \text{ then } x' \notin L(y)\}. \quad (1.39)$$

Then if input prices arc strictly positive, cost efficiency is accomplished with an efficient input vector. This may be verified following the same logic used for profit efficiency.

We measure technical efficiency via the **Directional Input Distance Function** which is defined as

$$\vec{D}_i(y, x; g_x) = \sup\{\beta : (x - \beta g_x) \in L(y)\} \quad (1.40)$$

and clearly this can be derived from the technology distance function $\vec{D}_T(x, y; g_x, g_y)$ by setting $g_y = 0$, thus

$$\vec{D}_i(y, x; g_x) = \vec{D}_T(x, y; g_x, 0) = \sup\{\beta : (x - \beta g_x) \in L(y)\}. \quad (1.41)$$

From this observation it is easy to deduce the following properties of the directional input distance function:

$\vec{\mathbf{D}}_{\mathbf{i}}$.1 $\vec{D}_i(y, x - \alpha g_x; g_x) = \vec{D}_i(y, x; g_x) - \alpha, \alpha \in \Re$, (**Translation**).

$\vec{\mathbf{D}}_{\mathbf{i}}$.2 $\vec{D}_i(y, x; \lambda g_x) = \lambda^{-1}\vec{D}_i(y, x; g_x), \lambda > 0$, (**Homogeneity of degree -1**).

$\vec{\mathbf{D}}_{\mathbf{i}}$.3 If inputs are strongly disposable, then $\vec{D}_i(y, x; g_x) \geqq 0$ if and only if $x \in L(y)$,
(**Representation**).

$\vec{\mathbf{D}}_{\mathbf{i}}$.4 If inputs are strongly disposable, then $\vec{D}_i(y, x; g_x)$ is nondecreasing in inputs.

$\vec{\mathbf{D}}_{\mathbf{i}}$.5 If outputs are strongly disposable, then $\vec{D}_i(y, x; g_x)$ is nonincreasing in outputs.

$\vec{\mathbf{D}}_{\mathbf{i}}$.6 If the technology exhibits constant returns to scale, i.e., $L(\lambda y) = \lambda L(y), \lambda > 0$, then $\vec{D}_i(\lambda y, \lambda x; g_x) = \lambda \vec{D}_i(y, x; g_x), \lambda > 0$.

Next we develop the connection between cost efficiency and technical efficiency. From the cost minimization problem in (1.38) we know that

$$C(y,w) \leqq wx \text{ for all } x \in L(y). \tag{1.42}$$

Thus since $(x - \vec{D}_i(y,x;g_x)g_x) \in L(y)$, we have

$$\frac{wx - C(y,w)}{wg_x} \geqq \vec{D}_i(y,x;g_x) \tag{1.43}$$

On the left hand side is the cost efficiency indicator and on the right hand side is the directional input distance function which we use here as a measure of technical efficiency.

As for our other indicators, we can add an allocative efficiency component to (1.43) to obtain the decomposition of cost efficiency into technical and allocative efficiency

$$CI(x,y,w;g_x) = \frac{wx - C(y,w)}{wg_x} = \vec{D}_i(y,x;g_x) + \vec{AE}_i. \tag{1.44}$$

As before, we may estimate the cost indicator and its components via simple linear programming problems. Let the input set be denoted by

$$\begin{aligned} L(y) = \{(x_1,\ldots,x_N) : \; & \sum_{k=1}^{K} z_k y_{km} \geqq y_m, m = 1,\ldots,M, \\ & \sum_{k=1}^{K} z_k x_{kn} \leqq x_n, n = 1,\ldots,N, \\ & z_k \geqq 0, k = 1,\ldots,K\}, \end{aligned} \tag{1.45}$$

which satisfies strong disposability of inputs and outputs, and exhibits constant returns to scale. Again the returns to scale could be readily modified to allow for variable returns to scale if that is deemed appropriate. See the production axiom appendix for details.

By solving the following linear programming problems

$$C(y,w) = \min\{wx : x \in L(y)\}$$

and

$$\vec{D}_i(y, x; g_x) = \max\{\beta : (x - \beta g_x) \in L(y)\}$$

we may compute cost efficiency and its component measures.

Finally Figure 1.10 illustrates the connections among our three efficiency indicators. Nerlovian profit efficiency is the general case; the revenue efficiency indicator and cost efficiency indicator are special cases. If we assume that observed cost is minimum cost and set the input direction vector equal to zero, then the Nerlovian profit efficiency indicator reduces to the revenue indicator. If instead we assume that observed revenue is equal to maximum revenue and set the output direction vector equal to zero, the Nerlovian profit efficiency indicator reduces to the cost indicator.

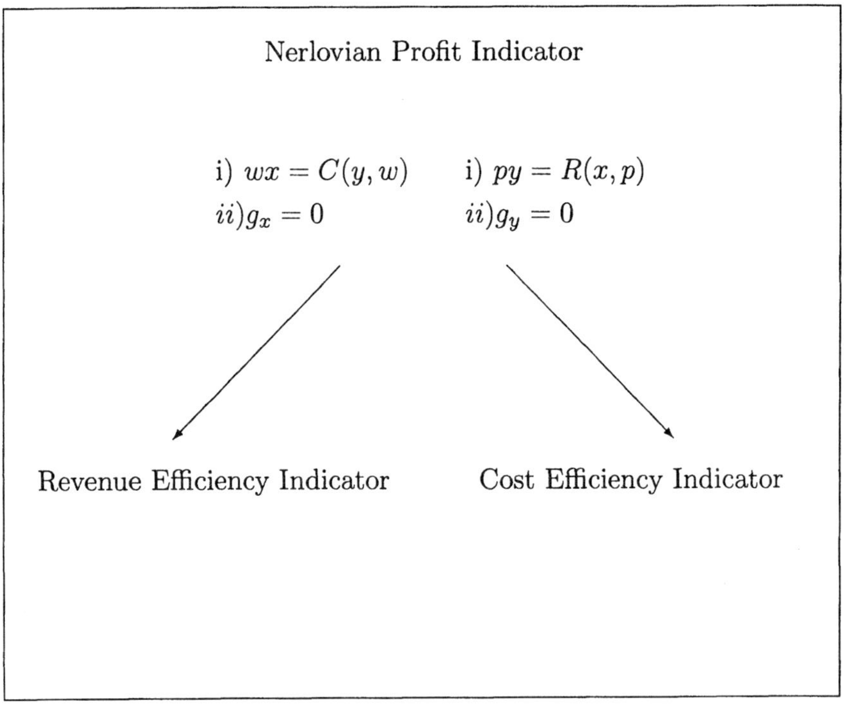

Figure 1.10. Relation Among Three Indicators

4. Efficiency Indexes

We now discuss efficiency indexes, which following Diewert (1998) are constructed as ratios rather than differences. Here we focus on the classic Farrell measures and their decompositions: cost efficiency and revenue efficiency. The indexes are ratios and the decompositions are multiplicative. This structure arises naturally from the duality between the distance functions and their associated support functions.

In his classic paper, Farrell (1957) defined cost efficiency as the ratio of minimum to observed or realized cost. He decomposed the index multiplicatively into a technical and allocative component. Although Farrell was probably not aware of it, his index and decomposition is an application of the Mahler (1939) inequality, which describes the duality between the distance function and its dual support function.

We have already discussed the cost function in the previous section, so we turn to its dual input distance function. Let the technology be represented by its input requirement sets $L(y) = \{x : x \text{ can produce } y\}, y \in \Re^M_+$, then Shephard's (1953) **Input Distance Function** is defined as

$$D_i(y,x) = \sup\{\lambda : x/\lambda \in L(y)\}. \tag{1.46}$$

The distance function seeks the maximal feasible contraction of the given input vector x, which is perhaps easiest to see in a diagram. In Figure 1.11, x^o is a feasible input vector, i.e., $x^o \in L(y)$. The distance function contracts x^o onto the boundary of $L(y)$ at $x^o/D_i(y,x^o)$. In the figure we see that the input vector $x^{'}$ is not feasible , i.e., $x^{'} \notin L(y)$. In this case the distance function expands $x^{'}$ radially until it attains the boundary of $L(y)$.

From its definition, the input distance function immediately inherits its **Homogeneity Property** in inputs (which has nothing to do with returns to scale):

D$_\mathbf{i}$.1 $D_i(y,\lambda x) = \lambda D_i(y,x), \lambda > 0.$

If inputs are weakly disposable (see the production axioms) then the distance function has following **Representation Property**.

D$_\mathbf{i}$.2 $D_i(y,x) \geqq 1$ if and only if $x \in L(y)$.

This property allows us to represent the technology equivalently by its input requirement sets or in terms of a function, namely

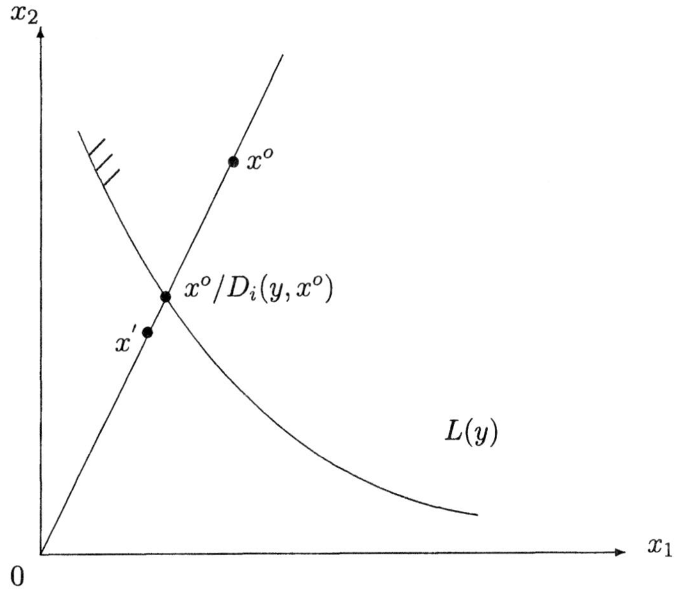

Figure 1.11. Input Distance Function

the input distance function.

If outputs are weakly disposable then the input distance function is **Ray-Nonincreasing** in outputs.

D_i.3 $D_i(\theta y, x) \leqq D_i(y, x), \theta \geqq 1.$

Under constant returns to scale, i.e., $L(\theta y) = \theta L(y), \theta > 0$, $D_i(y, x)$ is homogeneous of degree -1 in outputs

D_i.4 $D_i(\theta y, x) = \theta^{-1} D_i(y, x), \theta > 0.$

To develop the input oriented Mahler Inequality which is the basis for the cost efficiency decomposition, recall from the definition of the cost function that

$$C(y, w) \leqq wx \text{ for all } x \in L(y). \tag{1.47}$$

Now since $x/D_i(y, x) \in L(y)$, the Mahler inequality follows

$$\frac{C(y, w)}{wx} \leqq \frac{1}{D_i(y, x)}. \tag{1.48}$$

This inequality is the foundation for the input oriented measures of efficiency. The left hand side is the **Farrell Index of Cost Efficiency** $FC(y,x,w)$ and the right hand side is the input oriented **Farrell Index of Technical Efficiency** $F_i(y,x) = 1/D_i(y,x)$. The **Allocative Efficiency Index** $FA_i(y,x,w)$ is defined as the residual

$$FA_i(y,x,w) = \frac{C(y,w)D_i(y,x)}{wx}. \qquad (1.49)$$

Thus the input oriented Farrell approach to estimating and decomposing efficiency is summarized as follows

$$FC(y,x,w) = F_i(y,x)FA_i(y,x,w). \qquad (1.50)$$

We illustrate this in Figure 1.12.

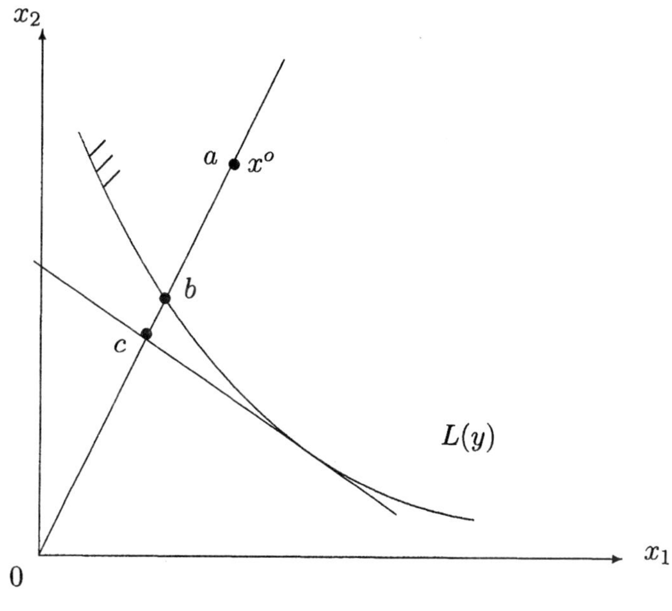

Figure 1.12. Farrell Input-Oriented Efficiency Indexes

The technology is represented by the input set $L(y)$, and the distance function contracts x^o from a to b and the corresponding Farrell technical efficency index is $0b/0a$. The ratio $0c/0b$ captures allocative inefficiency and $0c/0a$ gives the overall cost inefficiency due to both components.

In the previous section on cost indicators, we pointed out that if $C(y, w) - wx = 0$ for positive prices then x belongs to the efficient set $EffL(y)$, i.e., it is input efficient. Here, if x is a cost efficient input vector so that $FC(y, x, w) = 1$ then again x is input efficient. It remains to be seen whether the technical efficiency measure can be used to identify the efficient subset. To that end we first introduce the **Input Isoquant**

$$IsoqL(y) = \{x : x \in L(y), 0 < \lambda < 1, \lambda x \notin L(y)\}, y \in \Re_{+}^{M}. \tag{1.51}$$

From the definition of the distance function we know that

$$x \in IsoqL(y) \text{ if and only if } D_i(y, x) = 1. \tag{1.52}$$

Thus the **Indication Property** for the Farrell index of technical efficiency is

$$x \in IsoqL(y) \text{ if and only if } F_i(y, x) = 1. \tag{1.53}$$

Thus the technical efficiency measure can tell us whether an input vector is a member of the isoquant, but not necessarily whether it is a member of the efficient set.

As before, technical efficiency may be readily estimated as the solution to a simple linear programming problem. We assume that there are $k = 1, \ldots, K$ observations of inputs and outputs (x^k, y^k), then the input requirement set satisfying strong disposability and constant returns to scale for k' is

$$\begin{aligned} L(y^{k'}) = \{x : & \sum_{k=1}^{K} z_k y_{km} \geqq y_{k'm}, m = 1, \ldots, M, \\ & \sum_{k=1}^{K} z_k x_{kn} \leqq x_n, n = 1, \ldots, N, \\ & z_k \geqq 0, k = 1, \ldots, K\}. \end{aligned} \tag{1.54}$$

The Farrell technical efficiency input index can then be estimated as the solution to the linear programming problem for each observation k' as

$$F_i(y^{k'}, x^{k'}) = \min \lambda \tag{1.55}$$

$$\begin{aligned} s.t. \quad & \sum_{k=1}^{K} z_k y_{km} \geqq y_{k'm}, m = 1, \ldots, M, \\ & \sum_{k=1}^{K} z_k x_{kn} \leqq \lambda x_{k'n}, n = 1, \ldots, N, \\ & z_k \geqq 0, k = 1, \ldots, K. \end{aligned}$$

The estimation of the cost function in the activity analysis framework is as follows for each $k' = 1, \ldots, K$

$$\begin{aligned} C(w, y^{k'}, x^{k'}) \quad = \quad & \min_x wx \qquad (1.56) \\ s.t. \quad & \sum_{k=1}^{K} z_k y_{km} \geqq y_{k'm}, m = 1, \ldots, M, \\ & \sum_{k=1}^{K} z_k x_{kn} \leqq x_n, n = 1, \ldots, N, \\ & z_k \geqq 0, k = 1, \ldots, K. \end{aligned}$$

The constraints correspond to those in $L(y^{k'})$ above.

Next we turn to the output oriented Farrell approach to estimating efficiency. For the output orientation we focus on the output sets $P(x) = \{y : x \text{ can produce } y\}, x \in \Re_+^N$ as the representation of technology, and define Shephard's (1970) **Output Distance Function** as

$$D_o(x, y) \quad = \quad \inf\{\theta : y/\theta \in P(x)\}, \qquad (1.57)$$

i.e., it is defined as the maximum feasible expansion of the observed output vector y.

From its definition it follows that the output distance function has the following **Homogeneity Property**

D$_\mathbf{o}$.1 $D_o(x, \theta y) \quad = \quad \theta D_o(x, y), \theta > 0.$

If outputs are weakly disposable (see the production axioms) then the distance function has the following **Representation Property**

D$_\mathbf{o}$.2 $D_o(x, y) \leqq 1$ if and only if $y \in P(x)$.

Under constant returns to scale, the distance function is homogeneous of degree -1 in inputs,

$\mathbf{D_o.3}$ $D_o(\lambda x, y) = \lambda^{-1} D_o(x, y), \lambda > 0.$

Proofs of these properties are to be found in Färe and Primont (1995).

At this point it may be useful to point out the connection between the output distance function and the perhaps more familiar production function. Assuming a scalar output, the output set takes the form

$$P(x) = [0, F(x)], \tag{1.58}$$

where $F(x)$ is the production function. The distance function in this special case may be written

$$D_o(x, y) = y/F(x) \tag{1.59}$$

which may be interpreted as the ratio of observed to maximum feasible output.

Using the homogeneity property in output, we get

$$D_o(x, y) = yD_o(x, 1),$$

thus $1/D_o(x, 1))$ is a production function, i.e., $F(x) = 1/D_o(x, 1)$. Recall that the production function may also be interpreted as a directional output distance function, $F(x) = \vec{D}_o(x, 0; 1)$.

Turning to the revenue function, we know from its definition that

$$R(x, p) \geqq py \text{ for all } y \in P(x), \tag{1.60}$$

thus since $y/D_o(x, y) \in P(x)$ we obtain the **Mahler Inequality** for outputs

$$\frac{R(x, p)}{py} \geqq 1/D_o(x, y). \tag{1.61}$$

In words this inequality states that normalized maximum revenue is at least as large as the reciprocal of the output distance function, i.e., it is relating the primal distance function to its dual support function, i.e., the revenue function.

The left hand side may be called the **Farrell Index of Revenue Efficiency** $FR(x, y, p)$ and the right hand side is the output oriented **Farrell Index of Technical Efficiency** $F_o(x, y)$. We may close the Mahler Inequality by multiplying the right hand side with the output oriented **Farrell Index of Allocative Efficiency** $FA_o(x, y, p)$ to obtain

$$FR(x, y, p) = F_o(x, y) FA_o(x, y, p), \qquad (1.62)$$

where

$$FR(x, y, p) = R(x, p)/py,$$

$$F_o(x, y) = 1/D_o(x, y),$$

and

$$FA_o(x, y, p) = \frac{R(x, p) D_o(x, y)}{py}.$$

We illustrate the output oriented Farrell approach to efficiency measurement in Figure 1.13. The output set is denoted by $P(x)$ and the output vector to be evaluated is (y_1, y_2) at a. The revenue maximizing output vector is labeled (y_1^*, y_2^*) and at prices (p_1, p_2) maximum revenue is $R(x, p) = p_1 y_1^* + p_2 x_2^*$. The index of revenue efficiency $FR(x, y, p)$ is represented in the figure as $0c/0a$. Its technical component $F_o(x, y)$ is $0b/0a$ and its allocative component $FA_o(x, y, p)$ equals $0c/0b$.

In order to relate the efficiency properties of these indexes to our earlier defined indicators, recall that the output isoquant is defined as

$$IsoqP(x) = \{y : y \in P(x), \lambda > 1 \text{ implies that } \lambda y \notin P(x)\}. \qquad (1.63)$$

From the definition of the output distance function it follows that

$$y \in IsoqP(x) \text{ if and only if } D_o(x, y) = 1. \qquad (1.64)$$

Now since the measure of technical efficiency is the reciprocal of the distance function the Farrell index $F_o(x, y)$ has the following **Indication Property**

$$F_o(x, y) = 1 \text{ if and only if } y \in IsoqP(x). \qquad (1.65)$$

In words, the Farrell index of technical efficiency indicates efficiency if and only if the output vector belongs to the output isoquant. Again,

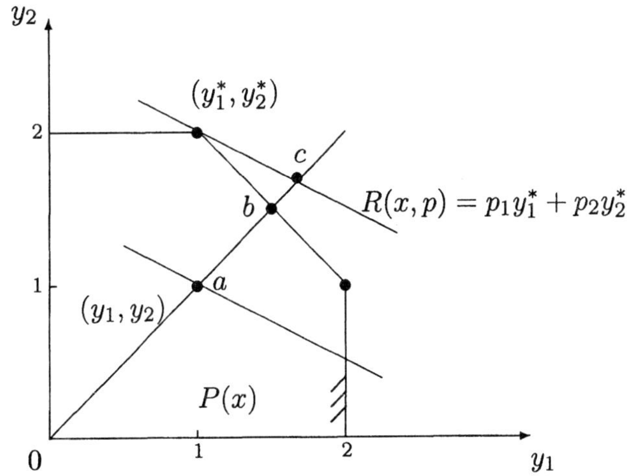

Figure 1.13. Farrell Output Oriented Efficiency Indexes

it does not necessarily belong to the efficient subset.

We showed earlier how one may estimate maximum revenue using linear programming methods; it remains to show how one may also estimate technical efficiency. Again assume that there are $k = 1, \ldots, K$ observation of inputs and outputs (x^k, y^k) and let the output set for observation k' satisfying strong disposability and constant returns to scale be given by

$$\begin{aligned} P(x^{k'}) \quad = \{y : \quad & \sum_{k=1}^{K} z_k y_{km} \geqq y_m, m = 1, \ldots, M, \\ & \sum_{k=1}^{K} z_k x_{kn} \leqq x_{k'n}, n = 1, \ldots, N, \\ & z_k \geqq 0, k = 1, \ldots, K\} \end{aligned} \tag{1.66}$$

The Farrell technical efficiency index (or its reciprocal the distance function) is obtained for each k' as the solution to the following linear programming problem

$$F_o(x^{k'}, y^{k'}) = (D_o(x^{k'}, y^{k'}))^{-1} = \max \theta \tag{1.67}$$

$$\begin{aligned} s.t. \quad & \sum_{k=1}^{K} z_k y_{km} \geqq \theta y_{k'm}, m = 1, \ldots, M, \\ & \sum_{k=1}^{K} z_k x_{kn} \leqq x_{k'n}, n = 1, \ldots, N, \\ & z_k \geqq 0, k = 1, \ldots, K. \end{aligned}$$

Here we have imposed strong disposability of inputs and outputs as well as constant returns to scale. These may be modified to suit the application under investigation.

5. From Indicators to Indexes

In the previous sections we discussed two approaches to estimating efficiency: the difference or indicator approach and the ratio or index approach. In this section we show how indexes can be derived from indicators. The key insight is that by choosing the appropriate directional vector, the Shephard distance functions arise as special cases from the more general directional distance function.

Recall the definition of the directional technology distance function

$$\vec{D}_T(x, y; g_x, g_y) = \sup\{\beta : (x - \beta g_x, y + \beta g_y) \in T\}. \quad (1.68)$$

If $g_x = 0$ then this function becomes the directional output distance function

$$\vec{D}_o(x, y; g_y). \quad (1.69)$$

Now if we choose the directional output vector g_y such that it is equal to the observed output vector y, i.e., $g_y = y$, then

$$\vec{D}_o(x, y; y) = 1/D_o(x, y) - 1. \quad (1.70)$$

Thus there is a simple relationship between the directional output distance function and the Shephard output distance function. To verify this, recall the representation property of the output distance function, i.e.,

$$D_o(x, y) \leqq 1 \text{ if and only if } y \in P(x).$$

This property together with the definition of the directional output distance function yields

$$\begin{aligned}
\vec{D}_o(x, y; y) &= \sup\{\beta : (y + \beta y) \in P(x)\} \qquad (1.71)\\
&= \sup\{\beta : D_o(x, y(1 + \beta)) \leqq 1\}\\
&= \sup\{\beta : D_o(x, y)(1 + \beta) \leqq 1\}\\
&= -1 + \sup\{(1 + \beta) : (1 + \beta) \leqq \frac{1}{D_o(x, y)}\}\\
&= -1 + \frac{1}{D_o(x, y)}
\end{aligned}$$

This proves our claim. Note that the homogeneity in y of the Shephard output distance function played a key role in this proof.

As we would expect, the input oriented measures have a similar relationship. If we choose $g_y = 0$ and $g_x = x$, then we can prove the following

$$\vec{D}_i(y, x; x) = 1 - 1/D_i(y, x). \qquad (1.72)$$

An example will help demonstrate the relationship between the two input-oriented distance functions.

Let the input requirement set take the following explicit form

$$L(y) = \{(x_1, x_2) : x_1 + x_2 \geqq y\}.$$

Let $y = 2, x_1 = 2$, and $x_2 = 1$. Then (x_1, x_2) belongs to $L(2)$, i.e., the input vector is feasible, see Figure 1.14.

Furthermore, if we choose the directional vector to be $-1 \cdot g_x = (-1, -1)$, then Figure 1.14 illustrates the directional input distance function for this technology and data.

In the figure we can see that the value of the directional distance function β^* is 1/2. If we change the direction vector to be -(2,1), i.e., the same value as the observed input bundle, but in the negative quadrant we get the following

$$\vec{D}_i(2, 2, 1; 2, 1) = \sup\{\beta : (2 - \beta 2) + (1 - \beta 1) \geqq 2\}$$

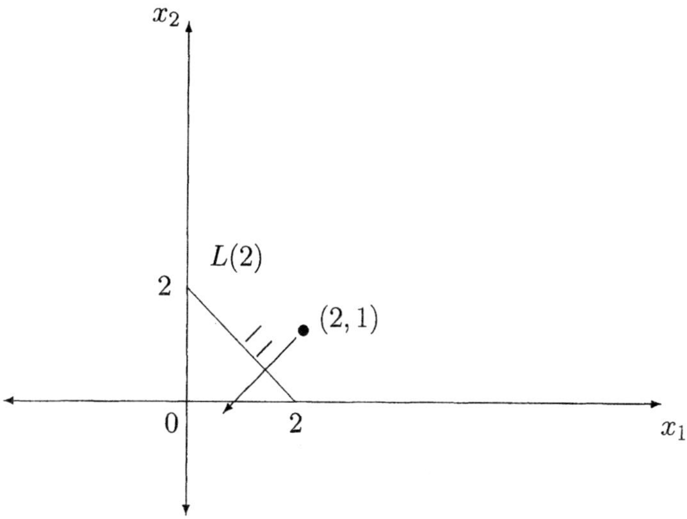

Figure 1.14. The Directional Input Distance Function

which is equal to 1/3.

If we calculate the Shephard distance function for the same data, we have

$$D_i(2,2,1) = \sup\{\lambda : \frac{2}{\lambda} + \frac{1}{\lambda} \geqq 2\}$$

the value is 3/2.

Thus we have

$$\vec{D}_i(2,2,1;2,1) = 1 - 2/3 = 1/3,$$

which is exactly the relationship derived earlier.

If we apply the results relating the directional and Shephard distance functions to the cost and revenue inequalities (1.43) and (1.31), respectively, then we retrieve the output and input-oriented Mahler inequalities. We demonstrate this for the output-oriented case. Recall that

$$\frac{R(x,p) - py}{pg_y} \geqq \vec{D}_o(x,y;g_y). \quad (1.73)$$

If we take $g_y = y$ and use the relationship between the two output oriented distance functions, then

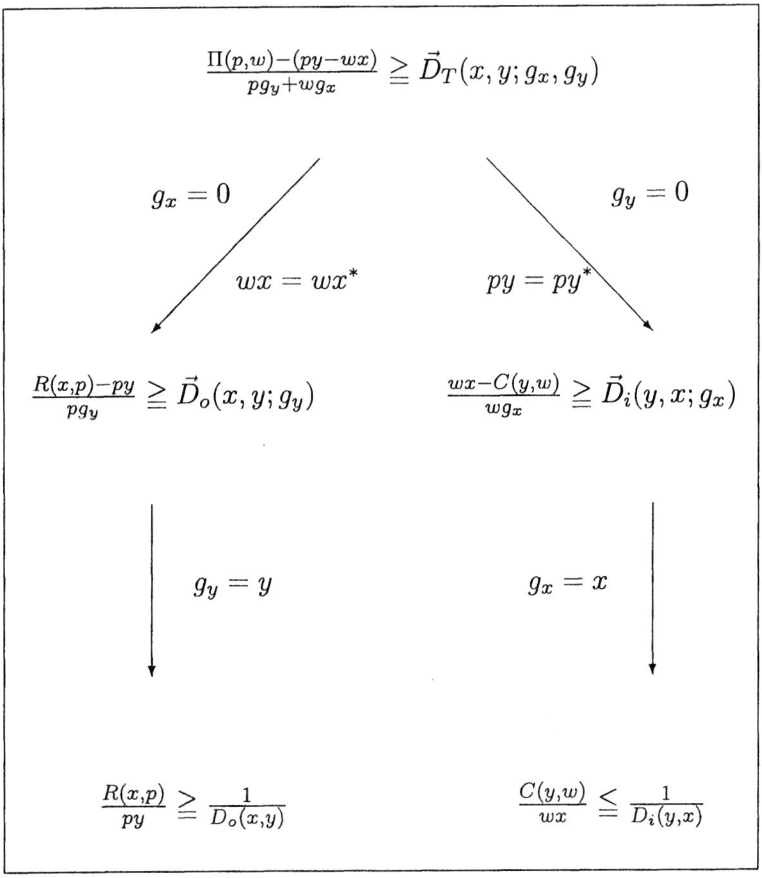

Figure 1.15. Efficiency Inequalities

$$\frac{R(x,p) - py}{py} \geqq \frac{1}{D_o(x,y)} - 1, \tag{1.74}$$

and upon simplification, the output-oriented Mahler inequality follows, i.e.,

$$\frac{R(x,p)}{py} \geqq \frac{1}{D_o(x,y)}. \tag{1.75}$$

The relationships among these inequalities may be summarized in a simple diagram, see Figure 1.15.

We start at the top with the most general case defined in terms of profit and directional distance functions; by restricting the directional vector we can derive revenue and cost inequalities in terms of directional distance functions. Finally, by restricting the direction to be equal to observed input or output, we derive the traditional multiplicative Mahler cost and revenue inequalities related to Shephard distance functions. In addition to the above five inequalities, there are two more that may prove useful. These inequalities relate the multiplicative Shephard distance functions with measures of profit efficiency. Thus we also have

$$\frac{\Pi(p,w)-(py-wx)}{py} \geqq \frac{1}{D_o(x,y)} - 1 \tag{1.76}$$

and

$$\frac{\Pi(p,w)-(py-wx)}{wx} \geqq 1 - \frac{1}{D_i(y,x)}. \tag{1.77}$$

The first inequality follows from

$$\frac{\Pi(p,w)-(py-wx)}{pg_y + wg_x} \geqq \vec{D}_T(x,y;g_x,g_y) \tag{1.78}$$

by taking $g_x = 0$ and $g_y = y$. The second inequality follows by setting $g_x = x$ and $g_y = 0$.

These inequalities may also be written as

$$\frac{\Pi(p,w)+wx}{py} \geqq \frac{1}{D_o(x,y)}$$

and

$$\frac{1}{D_i(y,x)} \geqq \frac{py - \Pi(p,w)}{wx},$$

which provide direct dual relationships between the profit function and the two Shephard distance functions.

6. Hyperbolic Efficiency and Return to the Dollar

As we have seen above, the Farrell or Debreu-Farrell measures of efficiency either expand outputs or contract inputs. The hyperbolic measure of efficiency scales on inputs and outputs simultaneously, but in contrast to the directional distance function it does so multiplicatively. To be precise, let T denote the technology, i.e., the set of (x,y) such that x can produce y. The **Technology Hyperbolic Distance Function** is defined as

$$H_T(x,y) = \inf\{\lambda : (\lambda x, y/\lambda) \in T\}. \tag{1.79}$$

The following figure illustrates.

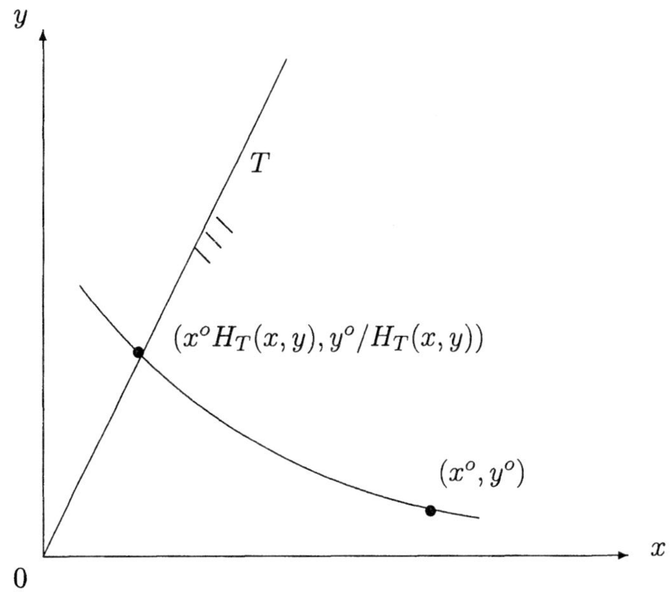

Figure 1.16. The Technology Hyperbolic Distance Function

The technology T is bounded by the $x-$axis and the ray from the origin. The hyperbolic measure projects the input output vector (x, y) onto the boundary of T by proportionally reducing inputs and proportionally expanding outputs.[2]

In this section we impose constant returns to scale (CRS) on the technology, i.e.,

$$\lambda T = T, \lambda > 0. \tag{1.80}$$

Equivalently

$$D_i(\lambda y, x) = \lambda^{-1} D_i(y, x), \lambda > 0. \tag{1.81}$$

[2]If we take a first order approximation to H_T we would have a directional technology distance function.

Using the input distance function's representation property

$$D_i(y,x) \geqq 1 \text{ if and only if } (x,y) \in T, \tag{1.82}$$

we can obtain a simple relationship between the input distance function and the hyperbolic distance function $H_T(x,y)$, namely

$$\begin{aligned} H_T(x,y) &= \inf\{\lambda : D_i(y/\lambda, \lambda x) \geqq 1\} \\ &= \inf\{\lambda : \lambda^2 \geqq 1/D_i(y,x)\} \\ &= (1/D_i(y,x))^{1/2} \end{aligned} \tag{1.83}$$

and hence

$$H_T(x,y) = (1/D_i(y,x))^{1/2}, \tag{1.84}$$

i.e., the hyperbolic distance function equals the square root of the reciprocal of the input distance function. Recall of course that we have assumed constant returns to scale, which also means that the output and input distance functions are reciprocal to each other, therefore we can rewrite the above relationship as

$$H_T(x,y) = D_o(x,y)^{1/2}, \tag{1.85}$$

To provide a dual representation of the hyperbolic measure, define **Return to the Dollar** as

$$\frac{py}{wx}. \tag{1.86}$$

This notion is due to Georgescu-Roegen (1951), and provides a ratio measure of revenue to cost, in contrast to the additive structure associated with profit. As it turns out, this ratio form is the natural partner to our multiplicative performance measures.

Under constant returns to scale, maximal profit is zero, i.e, $\Pi(p,w) = 0$, thus from the last expression in Section 1.5 we have

$$\frac{py}{wx} \leqq \frac{1}{D_i(y,x)} = (H_T(x,y))^2. \tag{1.87}$$

This says that under CRS, return to the dollar is dual to the hyperbolic technology distance function. Now if we introduce a residual term, namely hyperbolic allocative efficiency HA_T, i.e.,

$$HA_T = \frac{py}{wx} \frac{1}{(H_T(x,y))^2}, \tag{1.88}$$

we can specify the following decomposition of return to the dollar

$$\frac{py}{wx} = HA_T(H_T(x, y))^2, \tag{1.89}$$

where HA_T is allocative inefficiency and $(H_T(x, y))^2$ captures technical inefficiency.

7. Remarks on the Literature

Diewert (1998) introduced us to the distinction between indicators and indexes. Chambers, Chung and Färe (1998) generalized Nerlove's (1965) measure of profit efficiency with their Nerlovian profit indicator. The directional technology distance function introduced by Luenberger (1992,1995) was used as a component of the profit indicator. Luenberger refers to this as the shortage function. He also refers back to the Allais (1943) surplus function in the context of consumer theory. The directional output distance function was discussed by Chung (1996) in connection with modeling production with undesirable outputs.

Farrell (1957) and Debreu (1953) created the basic efficiency index models referred to here. These models can be seen as applications of the Mahler (1939) inequality, in which Shephard's (1953, 1970) or Malmquist's (1953) distance functions play the role as an index of technical efficiency. Färe and Grosskopf (2000) and Balk, Färe and Grosskopf (2004) analyze the relationships between indicators and indexes.

Färe, Grosskopf, Lovell and Pasurka (1989) introduced a hyperbolic distance function defined relative to the output set. Our discussion here follows Färe, Grosskopf and Zaim (2002). The concept of the return to the dollar is found in Georgescu-Roegen (1951) and it has also been discussed by Cooper, Seiford and Tone (2000).

8. Appendix: Proofs

PROOF OF PROPOSITION (1)
Suppose that (x, y) maximizes profit but is not efficient, then there exists a feasible vector (x', y') which has either some $x'_n < x_n$ or $y'_m > y_m$, thus since prices are strictly positive, $py' - wx' > py - wx$, contradicting the assumption that (x, y) maximizes profit.
Q.E.D.

PROOF OF $\vec{\mathbf{D}}_{\mathbf{T}}$.1.
$\vec{D}_T(x - \alpha g_x, y + \alpha g_y; g_x, g_y) = \sup\{\beta : (x - \alpha g_x - \beta g_x, y + \alpha g_y + \beta g_y) \in T\} = \sup\{\beta : x - (\alpha + \beta)g_x, y + (\alpha + \beta)g_y) \in T\} = -\alpha + \sup\{\alpha + \beta :$

$x - (\alpha + \beta)g_x, y + (\alpha + \beta)g_y) \in T\} = \vec{D}_T(x, y; g_x, g_y) - \alpha.$
Q.E.D.

PROOF OF $\vec{\mathbf{D}}_{\mathbf{T}}$.3.
Clearly if $(x, y) \in T$, $\vec{D}_T(x, y; g_x, g_y) \geqq 0$. Thus assume that $\vec{D}_T(x, y; g_x, g_y) \geqq 0$, then by definition $(x - \vec{D}_T(x, y; g_x, g_y)g_x, y + \vec{D}_T(x, y; g_x, g_y)g_y) \in T$. Since inputs and outputs are freely disposable, and $x \geqq x - \vec{D}_T(x, y; g_x, g_y)g_x, y \leqq y + \vec{D}_T(x, y; g_x, g_y)g_y$, therefore $(x, y) \in T$.
Q.E.D.

PROOF OF $\vec{\mathbf{D}}_{\mathbf{T}}$.6.
$\vec{D}_T(\lambda x, \lambda y; g_x, g_y) = \sup\{\beta : (\lambda x - \beta g_x, \lambda y + \beta g_y) \in T\} = \sup\{\beta/\lambda : (x - \beta/\lambda g_x, y + \beta/\lambda g_y) \in (1/\lambda)T\} = \lambda\vec{D}_T(x, y; g_x, g_y)$, since $(1/\lambda)T = T$.
Q.E.D.

The proofs of the other properties are left to the reader.

PROOF OF PROPOSITION (2)
Assume that a feasible vector $(x, y) \notin EffT$, then there exists $(x', y') \in T$ such that $(x - x', y' - y) \neq 0$. Take this difference as the directional vector, then for $\beta = 1$,
$(x - \beta(x - x'), y + \beta(y' - y)) \in T$
and hence $\vec{D}_T(x, y; g_x, g_y) > 0$.

To prove the second part assume that $(x, y) \in EffT$, then $(x - \beta g_x, y + \beta g_y) \notin T$ for any $(g_x, g_y) \neq 0$ and $\beta > 0$, thus $\vec{D}_T(x, y; g_x, g_y) = 0$.
Q.E.D.

PROOF OF PROPOSITIONS (3)-(5)
These are left to the reader.

Chapter 2

ESSAY 2: ENVIRONMENTAL PERFORMANCE

In this essay we give a selective overview of theory and application of modern axiomatic production theory and optimization models to the analysis of environmental issues. The overview is selective in that we focus on our own work in this area, which was originally motivated by the need to modify the traditional production model to accommodate the analysis of production when there are undesirable byproducts. That is the first issue we take up here—modifying the traditional axioms of production.

Those axioms have implications for the specification of technology, of course, which is what we take up next. Here we start with basic production sets modified to accommodate byproducts, then turn to function representations of technology—namely, distance functions. Since these may also serve as performance measures, we show how these may be modified to account for the fact that increases in byproducts are generally viewed to be undesirable.

Next we show how to use these basic building blocks—the distance functions—to provide us with some simple, but elegant, index numbers which can serve as basic environmental indicators for an industry or economy, for example. This basic index number approach can be elaborated to yield a productivity index which accounts for (and debits) the production of undesirable byproducts. We include an empirical application of this index to identification of an environmental Kuznets curve at the end of this essay.

Up to this point we have managed to model production with environmental effects and suggest measures of performance without appealing to prices. This is, of course, extremely useful when we are trying to analyze products which are typically not marketed. However, prices are extremely useful information as well. In fact, using our distance functions, and noting that they are dual to support functions such as profit, revenue or cost, we can retrieve underlying shadow prices of the undesirable, non marketed goods.

Finally, we would like to turn to what we refer to as network models. Here one may model externalities and spillovers within and across firms in a simple way, and simulate the effects of various property rights arrangements. We include an example of a network model applied to the case of an environmental externality, which we use to show the effect of various property rights arrangements on profitability.

1. Models with Good and Bad Outputs

In environmental economics one often wishes to distinguish between desirable ($y \in \Re^M_+$) and undesirable ($u \in \Re^J_+$) outputs. In the production context the former is typically a marketed good and the latter is often not marketed, but rather a byproduct which may have deleterious effects on the environment or human health, and therefore its disposal is often subject to regulation. Thus it may be useful to explicitly model the effects of producing both types of outputs, taking into account their characteristics and their interactions. Along these lines we introduce the ideas of **Null-Joint Outputs** and **Weak Disposability of Outputs**.

We begin with modeling the idea that desirable and undesirable outputs may be jointly produced, i.e., u is a byproduct of the production of y. Here we are thinking of, for example, electricity generated from a coal-fired utility. In this case the desirable, marketed output is Kwh of electricity, one undesirable byproduct is SO_2 (others may include particulates and NO_x). The basic environmental problem is that given technology, producing electricity means simultaneously producing SO_2, even though its production is undesirable. Specifically we say that the desirable output vector y is **Null-Joint** with the undesirable outputs u if

$$(y, u) \in P(x), \text{ and } u = 0 \text{ then } y = 0. \tag{2.1}$$

In other words if an output vector (y, u) is feasible and there are no bad outputs produced, then under null jointness only zero good output can be produced. Equivalently if some positive amount of the good output is produced then some bad output must also be produced.

What this means is that if we were to draw a production possibility set with one good output y and a single bad output u, if they are null joint, then the only part of the good output axis which is feasible is the origin (null).

In terms of disposability, we have two alternative assumptions concerning output disposability:

$$(y, u) \in P(x) \text{ and } 0 \leqq \theta \leqq 1, \text{ imply } (\theta y, \theta u) \in P(x). \tag{2.2}$$

$$(y^o, u^o) \in P(x) \text{ and } (y, u) \leqq (y^o, u^o), \text{ imply } (y, u) \in P(x). \tag{2.3}$$

Expression (2.2) imposes **Weak Disposability of Outputs** on the technology and it says that if a feasible output vector $(y, u) \in P(x)$ is proportionally decreased then it is still feasible, i.e, $(\theta y, \theta u) \in P(x)$, where $0 \leqq \theta \leqq 1$. If desirable and undesirable outputs are jointly produced, and the undesirable output may not be disposed of costlessly (perhaps via regulatory restrictions) then (2.2) is an appropriate assumption on the technology since it says that if undesirable outputs are to be decreased then (at the margin) the desirable outputs must also be decreased, holding inputs x constant. An alternative interpretation is that if we hold inputs constant, then 'cleaning up' undesirable outputs will occur at the margin through reallocation of inputs away from the production of desirable outputs.

Strong or Free Disposability (2.3) allows any output to be disposed of costlessly. Clearly this assumption would be inappropriate for technologies in which undesirable outputs such as SO_2 emissions cannot be costlessly disposed into the environment, because of regulation for example. If there is joint production of desirable and regulated, undesirable outputs, one may allow for free disposability of the subvector of desirable outputs, while imposing weak disposability on the vector of desirable and undesirable outputs jointly. To see this we treat desirable outputs y and undesirable outputs u asymmetrically. Now if $(y^o, u^o) \in P(x)$ and $y \leqq y^o$ (but u is held constant at u^o), then it should be the case that $(y, u^o) \in P(x)$, i.e., the desirable outputs could be disposed of costlessly. Note, that (2.3) implies (2.2) but that the converse is not true.

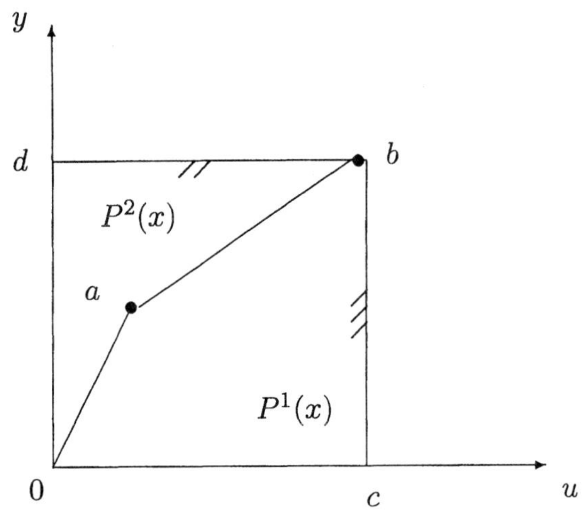

Figure 2.1. Weak and Strong Disposability of Outputs

Figure 2.1 illustrates the two disposability assumptions (2.2) and (2.3).

In this figure two different output sets are illustrated. The first is $P^1(x)$ which consists of the area bounded by $0abc0$ and the second is $P^2(x)$ which is bounded by $0dbc0$. The first output set satisfies weak disposability of outputs since any element (y, u) in $P^1(x)$ can be proportionally contracted (scaled toward the origin) and still remain in the set. On the other hand, this set does not satisfy strong or free disposability since a point like d represents an output vector smaller than the output vector b (which belongs to $P^2(x)$), yet d does not belong to $P^1(x)$. The output set $P^2(x)$, however, does satisfy strong disposability. The discrepancy between the two sets may be thought of as a characterization of the effect or effectiveness of regulation, i.e., the degree to which regulation prevents free disposability of undesirable outputs.

In this figure we can also see that for the $P^1(x)$ technology, if $u = 0$ then the only feasible production of good output is $y = 0$, i.e., this technology exhibits null-jointness.

Before we begin to employ these basic modifications in technology to address performance issues in the presence of externalities or bads, we note that instead of using the notions we have introduced above to integrate the production of undesirables into the model, many others instead treat undesirables as 'inputs'. This has intuitive appeal; inputs and undesirables—at least in the presence of regulation—are 'costly', although inputs generally require out of pocket costs. Nevertheless, we would still like to maintain the conceptualization of undesirables as outputs. For example, think of an isoquant between an undesirable and an input–suppose we choose SO_2 and coal as in our electric utility example. A traditional isoquant would suggest that these two should be substitutable, i.e., we should be able to produce a given level of power with some combination of SO_2 and coal, and we should be able to produce that same level of power by reducing say coal by some amount by substituting additional amounts of SO_2 (holding all else constant). Of course, this is not technically feasible, since the coal is the source of the SO_2.

We also find the idea of modeling undesirables as inputs problematic in the sense that typically we think of inputs as strongly disposable, and that the production set is not bounded in those inputs—think of a total product curve with input on the horizontal axis and output on the vertical axis. Unlimited increases in undesirables (holding other inputs constant) is not technically possible; it also violates our assumption that the output sets are bounded.

There are several ways of integrating our alternate assumptions of null jointness and weak disposability into a representation of technology, including nonparametric and parametric approaches. Here we focus on the nonparametric model using activity analysis or DEA. We defer our discussion of the parametric approach to the section on shadow pricing.

We assume that there are $k = 1, \ldots, K$ observations of inputs and outputs

$$(x^k, y^k, u^k). \tag{2.4}$$

Based on this data we may construct the technology, here represented by the output set $P(x)$. Specifically, for observation k' we have

$$\begin{aligned} P(x^{k'}) \quad &= \quad \{(y,u) : \\ &\sum_{k=1}^{K} z_k y_{km} \geqq y_m, m = 1, \ldots, M, \\ &\sum_{k=1}^{K} z_k u_{kj} \quad = \quad u_j, j = 1, \ldots, J, \end{aligned} \tag{2.5}$$

$$\sum_{k=1}^{K} z_k x_{kn} \leqq x_{k'n}, n = 1, \ldots, N,$$
$$z_k \geqq 0, k = 1, \ldots, K\}.$$

The constraint for the undesirable outputs $u_j = 1, \ldots, J$ are equality constraints, which under constant returns to scale models the idea that these outputs are not freely disposable. We allow for free disposability of the inputs and desirable outputs, however, which is imposed by the inequalities in their respective constraints.

To demonstrate that this technology allows for outputs to be weakly disposable, let $(y, u) \in P(x^{k'})$ and let $0 < \theta \leqq 1$, then we need to show that

$$(\theta y, \theta u) \in P(x^{k'}), \tag{2.6}$$

i.e., that

$$\begin{aligned}
\sum_{k=1}^{K} z_k y_{km} &\geqq \theta y_m, \quad m = 1, \ldots, M, \\
\sum_{k=1}^{K} z_k u_{kj} &= \theta u_j, \quad j = 1, \ldots, J, \\
\sum_{k=1}^{K} z_k x_{kn} &\leqq x_{k'n}, \quad n = 1, \ldots, N, \\
z_k &\geqq 0, \quad k = 1, \ldots, K
\end{aligned}$$

is feasible.

It follows that

$$\begin{aligned}
\sum_{k=1}^{K} (z_k/\theta) y_{km} &\geqq y_m, m = 1, \ldots, M, \\
\sum_{k=1}^{K} (z_k/\theta) u_{kj} &= u_j, j = 1, \ldots, J, \\
\sum_{k=1}^{K} (z_k/\theta) x_{kn} &\leqq (x_{k'n}/\theta), n = 1, \ldots, N,
\end{aligned}$$

$$(z_k/\theta) \geqq 0/\theta \;=\; 0, k = 1, \ldots, K.$$

Now since $(z_k/\theta) \geqq 0)$ and $(x_{k'n}/\theta) \geqq x_{k'n}, n \;=\; 1, \ldots, N$, and since $(\theta y, \theta u) \in P(x^{k'})$ for $\theta = 0$, the technology satisfies weak disposability of outputs.

In the proof that model (2.5) satisfies weak disposability of outputs, two conditions were employed. First, the technology we use satisfies constant returns to scale, which allows us to use the intensity variables $(z_k/\theta), k = 1, \ldots, K$, to 'scale' the good and undesirable outputs. Second, we exploit the assumption that inputs are at least weakly disposable (recall that strong disposability implies weak disposability, see Appendix) so that scaling on $(x_{k'n}/\theta), n = 1, \ldots, N$ will not reduce output. Since all of our models in this essay allow for inputs to be at least weakly disposable, we focus on issues concerning relaxation of constant returns to scale.

If we impose variable returns to scale (VRS) on the production model in (2.5) by restricting the intensity variables to sum to one, i.e., $\sum_{k=1}^{K} z_k = 1, z_k \geqq 0, k = 1, \ldots, K$, then we need to modify the constraints on the desirable and undesirable outputs. Specifically, we introduce a scaling factor $\delta \geqq 1$ and rewrite these constraints as

$$\sum_{k=1}^{K} z_k y_{km} \geqq \delta y_{km}, m \;=\; 1, \ldots, M,$$

$$\sum_{k=1}^{K} z_k u_{kj} \;=\; \delta u_{kj}, j \;=\; 1, \ldots, J.$$

With this modification our technology satisfies weak disposability of good and bad outputs together, strong disposability of good outputs and VRS.

To impose null-jointness in this model, the data or technology coefficients need to satisfy the following conditions.

$$\sum_{k=1}^{K} u_{kj} > 0, j = 1, \ldots, J, \tag{2.7}$$

$$\sum_{j=1}^{J} u_{kj} > 0, k = 1, \ldots, K. \tag{2.8}$$

The first set of inequalities says that each bad output is produced by at least one observation. The second set of inequalities states that each firm produces at least one bad output.

To verify that the conditions (2.7) and (2.8) above imply that good and bad outputs are null-joint, set $u_j, j = 1, \ldots, J$ equal to zero on the right-hand-side of the bad output constraints. Then, given the two conditions above, each $z_k = 0, k = 1, \ldots, K$ in order for the constraints in the model to hold, and hence the right hand side of the good output constraints must satisfy $y_m = 0, m = 1, \ldots, M$; thus we have established that the two sets of conditions imply null-jointness.

Normally we would expect that effective regulation would yield output quantity data that reflects weak disposability of good and bad outputs (and possibly strong disposability of the good outputs); thus weak disposability may be used to indirectly model regulation of undesirable outputs. However, one may also have explicit information on regulatory rules, which may be included in constructing the technology. For example, an industry may have firm specific limits on emissions of specific undesirable outputs, which could be included as explicit constraints in the model above.

In the next sections we demonstrate how this technology may be used to measure environmental performance.

2. Productivity in the Presence of Undesirable Outputs

In response to the joint production of undesirable outputs which are not marketable, regulators and lawmakers may intervene in the market in order to restrict production of these undesirables. These restrictions typically increase the costs of production directly or indirectly, *ceteris paribus.*[1] Because the undesirable outputs are not marketed, the firm is typically not credited with reductions in them when their performance is evaluated using standard productivity and efficiency measures. Thus firms that are complying with environmental standards by installing scrubbers, for example, would look less efficient than firms that do not, since they are not given credit for the reduction in emissions. The purpose of this section is to provide measures of performance that directly

[1] We do not consider the Porter hypothesis directly here which suggests that environmental regulations foster technical change, although one can imagine using the techniques we propose to test the hypothesis.

account for reductions in undesirable outputs.

Since the undesirable outputs are typically not marketed, there are no readily available prices. This means that the standard dual models such as revenue and profit functions would be difficult to apply here without independently estimating shadow prices, for example. Instead we adopt primal models which rely on quantity data here. Shadow pricing is taken up later in this Essay.

As discussed in Essay 1 there are a number of primal models, including radial distance functions and (additive) directional distance functions. Since we wish to explicitly account for the reduction of undesirable outputs, a directional output distance function with an appropriately chosen direction to reduce undesirable outputs seems appropriate. Let us consider such a function with the direction vector (g_y, g_u)

$$\vec{D}_o(x, y, u; g_y, g_u) = \max\{\beta : (y + \beta g_y, u - \beta g_u) \in P(x)\}. \qquad (2.9)$$

This distance function seeks the largest feasible expansion of desirable output in the g_y direction and the largest feasible contraction of undesirable output in the g_u direction.

We illustrate the directional output distance function with good and bad outputs in the following figure. Here we have imposed our assumptions of null-joint production and weak disposability of good and bad outputs, and strong disposability of the desirable output y. In this figure the observation (y, u) at c is projected in the direction b, i.e., in the direction of reduced u and increased y, onto the boundary of technology. In our particular case the direction b is also $(g_y, g_u) = (y, u)$; it is the translated value of the observation (y, u). The value of the distance function for this observation is $0a/0b$.

Based on this particular distance function one can construct a productivity indicator which simultaneously accounts for the joint production of desirable and undesirable outputs, crediting for increased desirable output and debiting increases in undesirables. Since the distance function itself has an additive structure, we construct the productivity indicator in a similar way, i.e., in terms of differences rather than ratios. The indicator introduced here is an output-oriented version of **The Luenberger Productivity Indicator** introduced by Chambers (1996).

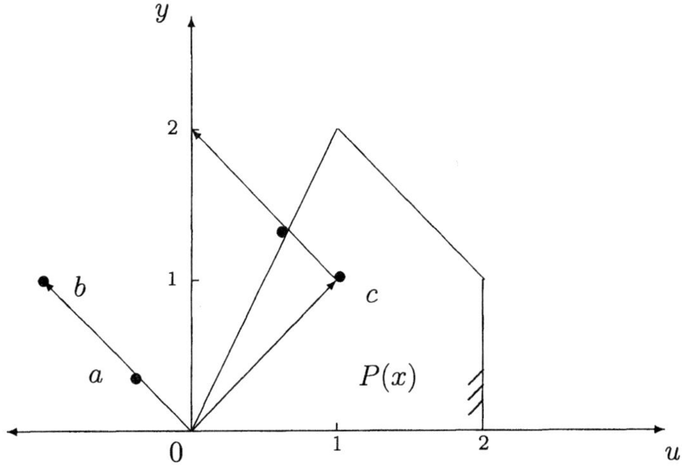

Figure 2.2. Directional output distance function with good and bad outputs

In order to define productivity change, we modify our directional distance functions to be time dependent; i.e., we compare performance in adjacent periods, t and $t+1$. Specifically, we have

$$\begin{aligned} \mathcal{L}_t^{t+1} &= 1/2(\vec{D}_o^{t+1}(x^t, y^t, u^t; g_y, g_u) \\ &-\vec{D}_o^{t+1}(x^{t+1}, y^{t+1}, u^{t+1}; g_y, g_u) \\ &+\vec{D}_o^t(x^t, y^t, u^t; g_y, g_u) - \vec{D}_o^t(x^{t+1}, y^{t+1}, u^{t+1}; g_y, g_u)). \end{aligned} \tag{2.10}$$

Here $\vec{D}_o^{t+1}$ means that the reference technology is constructed from data from period $t+1$ and the data being evaluated is included in the parentheses with its associated time period; for example (x^t, y^t, u^t) would mean that the data to be evaluated are from period t. We assume that the direction vector (g_y, g_u) is time independent and the same for all periods.

Following the idea of Chambers, Färe and Grosskopf (1996) the Luenberger productivity indicator can be additively decomposed into an efficiency change and a technical change component,

$$LECH_t^{t+1} = \vec{D}_o^t(x^t, y^t, u^t; g_y, g_u) - \vec{D}_o^{t+1}(x^{t+1}, y^{t+1}, u^{t+1}; g_y, g_u)$$

and

$$LTCH_t^{t+1} = 1/2[\vec{D}_o^{t+1}(x^{t+1}, y^{t+1}, u^{t+1}; g_y, g_u) \tag{2.11}$$

$$-\vec{D}_o^t(x^{t+1}, y^{t+1}, u^{t+1}; g_y, g_u) + \vec{D}_o^{t+1}(x^t, y^t, u^t; g_y, g_u)$$
$$-\vec{D}_o^t(x^t, y^t, u^t; g_y, g_u)],$$

respectively. The sum of these two components equals the Luenberger productivity indicator.

Our indicator and its components signal improvements with values greater than zero, and declines in productivity with values less than zero.[2] As usual, it is up to the researcher to choose the directional vector for empirical purposes. If we choose $(g_y, g_u) = (y, u)$, i.e., choose the observed good, bad output vector to determine the direction, then each observation may be evaluated in a different direction—just as is typically the case for Shephard type distance functions. If one chooses a common direction for all observations, then aggregation is facilitated as is discussed in Essay 3.

To estimate the Luenberger indicator requires estimation of the component directional output distance functions. As in Essay 1, this may be easily accomplished using activity analysis models. As before we assume that we have $k = 1, \ldots, K$ observations, but in our case we have both desirable outputs y and undesirable outputs u, plus we have two periods t and $t+1$. Finally, we also wish to impose null-jointness and weak disposability. Let us suppose that we wish to estimate $\vec{D}_o^{t+1}(x^t, y^t, u^t; g_y, g_u)$, for observation k'. This is accomplished with the following linear programming problem

$$\begin{aligned} \vec{D}_o^{t+1}(x^{k',t}, y^{k',t}, u^{k',t}; g_y, g_u) &= \max \beta \qquad (2.12) \\ s.t. \sum_{k=1}^{K} z_k^{t+1} y_{km}^{t+1} &\geq y_{k'm}^t + \beta g_{y_m}, m = 1, \ldots, M, \\ \sum_{k=1}^{K} z_k^{t+1} u_{kj}^{t+1} &= u_{k'j}^t - \beta g_{u_j}, j = 1, \ldots, J, \end{aligned}$$

[2]To see this for LECH, for example, note that feasible values of the directional distance function take values greater than or equal to zero, thus both $\vec{D}_o^t(x^t, y^t, u^t; g_y, g_u)$ and $\vec{D}_o^{t+1}(x^{t+1}, y^{t+1}, u^{t+1}; g_y, g_u)$ will be greater than or equal to zero. If the data are closer to the frontier in period $t+1$ than period t, then $\vec{D}_o^{t+1}(x^{t+1}, y^{t+1}, u^{t+1}; g_y, g_u) < \vec{D}_o^t(x^t, y^t, u^t; g_y, g_u)$ and their difference $\vec{D}_o^t(x^t, y^t, u^t; g_y, g_u) - \vec{D}_o^{t+1}(x^{t+1}, y^{t+1}, u^{t+1}; g_y, g_u)$ will be greater than zero, signaling that efficiency has improved.

$$\sum_{k=1}^{K} z_k^{t+1} x_{kn}^{t+1} \leqq x_{k'n}^{t}, n = 1, \ldots, N,$$
$$z_k^{t+1} \geqq 0, k = 1, \ldots, K.$$

In this problem, data for observation k' in period t is evaluated in the (g_y, g_u) direction. The subscripts on the direction vector account for the possibility of multiple good and multiple undesirable outputs, and the undesirable output direction is such that we wish to reduce these outputs. Weak disposability is imposed through the strict equality in the undesirable output constraints. Note also that the superscripts on the left-hand-side are $t + 1$; these form the reference technology for the period $t + 1$ relative to which the data for observation k' from period t (on the right hand side) are compared. The three other directional distance functions are derived similarly by varying the time superscripts and making the proper substitutions. Each of these functions satisfy the translation property discussed in Essay 1.

We would argue that the Luenberger productivity indicator, by explicitly debiting increases in undesirable outputs, provides a more accurate summary of productivity change in the presence of joint production of desirable and undesirable outputs than conventional measures which typically ignore undesirables. The Luenberger indicator does not explicitly sort out whether any gains in productivity are due to increases in desirable outputs, decreases in undesirable outputs or some combination. This is in part due to the fact that the Luenberger indicator as constructed here is not separable in the good and bad outputs. The next section turns to an approach that allows such an identification.

3. A Quantity Index Approach to Environmental Performance

If we think of distance functions as aggregator functions, then it follows that they are the perfect building blocks for constructing quantity indexes. Indeed, that is exactly what Malmquist originally proposed in his 1953 paper in the context of the consumer. Here we show how to use Shephard type distance functions to construct fairly simple environmental performance indexes that show whether an observation has improved in terms of its ability to produce good relative to bad output, either over time or relative to some benchmark.

We begin by maintaining our assumptions concerning null-jointness and weak disposability. Given those assumptions we can define 'subvector' distance functions for the desirable and undesirable outputs. These in turn are combined to form our environmental index. Begin with a subvector distance function for the desirable outputs specified as

$$D_y(x, y, u) = \inf\{\theta : (x, y/\theta, u) \in T\} \qquad (2.13)$$

where good output y is expanded as much as is feasible given (x, u) and the technology T. By definition, this function is homogeneous of degree $+1$ in y. Let x^o and u^o be our given levels of inputs and undesirable outputs, then we can construct a quantity index of good outputs by comparing two output vectors, say y^k and y^l using our distance functions:

$$Q_y(x^o, u^o, y^k, y^l) = \frac{D_y(x^o, y^k, u^o)}{D_y(x^o, y^l, u^o)} \qquad (2.14)$$

This quantity index satisfies a number of Fisher's (1922) tests, including homogeneity, time reversal, transitivity, and dimensionality.

Homogeneity tells us that

$$Q_y(x^o, u^o, \lambda y^k, y^l) = \lambda Q_y(x^o, u^o, y^k, y^l), \lambda > 0.$$

Time Reversal means that

$$Q_y(x^o, u^o, y^k, y^l) \cdot Q_y(x^o, u^o, y^l, y^k) = 1.$$

Transitivity, also known as the circular test, holds if

$$Q_y(x^o, u^o, y^k, y^l) \cdot Q_y(x^o, u^o, y^l, y^s) = Q_y(x^o, u^o, y^k, y^s).$$

Finally, **Dimensionality** states that

$$Q_y(x^o, u^o, \lambda y^k, \lambda y^l) = Q_y(x^o, u^o, y^k, y^l), \lambda > 0.$$

These conditions depend on the reference vector (x^o, u^o); below we provide conditions on the technology such that our indexes are independent of the choice of reference vector.

Similarly, we may construct a quantity index of bad outputs based on distance functions which satisfies conditions similar to those itemized above. In this case the distance function contracts the undesirable output as much as is feasible given y and x, i.e.,

$$D_u(x, y, u) = \sup\{\lambda : (x, y, u/\lambda) \in T\}, \qquad (2.15)$$

and the associated quantity index of undesirable outputs may be written as

$$Q_u(x^o, y^o, u^k, u^l) = \frac{D_u(x^o, y^o, u^k)}{D_u(x^o, y^o, u^l)}. \tag{2.16}$$

As mentioned above, this quantity index also satisfies the Fisher tests described earlier.

Taking these two quantity indexes together, following Färe, Grosskopf and F. Hernandez-Sancho (2004) we can define the **Environmental Performance Index** as

$$E^{k,l}(x^o, y^o, u^o, y^k, y^l, u^k, u^l) = \frac{Q_y(x^o, u^o, y^k, y^l)}{Q_u(x^o, y^o, u^k, u^l)}. \tag{2.17}$$

Intuitively, this gives us an index of how much good output is produced per unit of bad output. Clearly, larger values are 'better' as long as u is undesirable. By inspecting the component quantity indexes, one may determine if the environmental index is improving due to relatively fast growth in desirable outputs, declines in undesirable outputs or some combination of the two. The fact that the overall index and its components are based on distance functions also means that we are explicitly taking technology and resources into account.

The environmental performance index inherits its properties from the 'good' and 'bad' indexes. As the ratio of these indexes, it satisfies the same Fisher tests as its component indexes. In the case when only one good and one bad output are produced the performance index takes the following simple form due to the homogeneity of the underlying distance functions

$$E^{k,l} = \frac{y^l/y^k}{u^l/u^k} = \frac{y^l/u^l}{y^k/u^k}. \tag{2.18}$$

This allows us to see that our index may also be interpreted as a simple productivity type index measuring the change in the average good per bad output production.

In estimating the performance index one must choose a reference vector (x^o, y^o, u^o), or one may ask under what conditions the index is independent of the choice of the reference vector. In our application of this index in Section 6 we estimate the index by setting the reference vector equal to the observed value of the data in 1971. Here we show when the good and bad indexes are independent of that vector, i.e., when it is base invariant.

We begin by considering what properties the technology (distance function) must satisfy for the good index to be base invariant, i.e, for the following to hold

$$\frac{D_y(x^o, y^k, u^o)}{D_y(x^o, y^l, u^o)} = \frac{D_y(x^1, y^k, u^1)}{D_y(x^1, y^l, u^1)}. \tag{2.19}$$

One can show (see Appendix) that a necessary and sufficient condition for (2.19) to be satisfied is that

$$D_y(x^o, y^k, u^o) = \frac{D_y(x^o, 1, u^o)}{D_y(1, 1, 1)} D_y(1, y^k, 1). \tag{2.20}$$

In this case the good index can be written as

$$Q_y(x^o, u^o, y^k, y^l) = \frac{D_y(1, y^k, 1)}{D_y(1, y^l, 1)} = Q_y(y^k, y^l). \tag{2.21}$$

If we assume that the distance function $D_y(1, y, 1)$ may be written as a homogeneous translog function, i.e.,

$$\ln D_y(1, y, 1) = \alpha_o + \sum_{m=1}^{M} \alpha_m \ln y_m + (1/2) \sum_{m=1}^{M} \sum_{m'=1}^{M} \beta_{mm'} \ln y_m \ln y_{m'}$$

where

$$\sum_{m=1}^{M} \alpha_m = 1, \beta_{mm'} = \beta_{m'm}, \sum_{m'=1}^{M} \beta_{mm'} = 0, m = 1, \ldots, M,$$

then Diewert (1993, p. 228) has shown that if revenue maximization is assumed then (2.21) can be written as

$$Q_y(y^k, y^l) = \Pi_{m=1}^{M} (y_{km}/y_{lm})^{1/2(s_{km}+s_{lm})}. \tag{2.22}$$

The revenue shares are given by $s_{km} = p_{km}y_{km}/(p^k y^k)$ and $s_{lm} = p_{lm}y_{lm}/(p^l y^l)$, respectively, where p_{km} is the price of output m for observation k.

The quantity index (2.22) is the Törnqvist index, named after Törnqvist (1936). Note that this index requires that output quantities be strictly positive.

Turning to the bad quantity index, we can repeat the process above and show that for the index to be independent of the reference (x^o, y^o), the distance function must take the form

$$D_u(x^o, y^o, u^k) = \frac{D_u(x^o, y^o, 1)}{D_u(1,1,1)} D_u(1,1,u^k). \tag{2.23}$$

Also if we assume that $D_u(1,1,u^k)$ is a homogeneous translog function and that r_{kj} is the shadow price of the j'th bad output for observation k and revenue maximization holds then we may write the bad index as a Törnqvist index

$$Q_u(u^k, u^l) = \Pi_{j=1}^{J} (u_{kj}/u_{lj})^{1/2(r_{kj}u_{kj}/(r^k u^k) + r_{lj}u_{lj}/(r^l u^l))}. \tag{2.24}$$

If we take (2.22) and (2.24) together to form our environmental performance index we see that it is a ratio of two Törnqvist indexes, one for desirable and one for undesirable outputs. This index reduces to our simple ratios of good to bad output in the single good, single bad case.

In the next section we show how one may estimate the shadow prices for the nonmarketed, undesirable outputs.

4. Shadow Pricing Undesirable Outputs

As we have mentioned earlier, in general there are no markets for undesirable outputs, thus their prices must be estimated. Obviously, the readily available data is primal or quantity data. A natural approach, then, is to appeal to duality, i.e., use the primal data to estimate the dual shadow prices. The duality that we appeal to here is between the revenue function and the associated output distance functions. The two candidate distance functions are the Shephard output distance function and the directional output distance function. Recall that the Shephard distance function seeks to radially expand all outputs proportionally, with the implication that more of all outputs is desirable. Obviously, this is not what we wish to do with undesirable outputs; rather we would like to reduce them. This leads us naturally to adopt the directional output distance function, which allows for simultaneous expansion of good outputs and contraction of undesirable outputs.

Let $g = (g_y, g_u)$ be a directional vector such that the good outputs are expanded and the undesirable outputs are contracted. The directional output distance function is defined as

$$\vec{D}_o(x, y, u; g_y, g_u) = \max\{\beta : (y + \beta g_y, u - \beta g_u) \in P(x)\}. \tag{2.25}$$

Furthermore define the revenue function as

$$R(x, p, r) = \max\{py - ru : (y, u) \in P(x)\}, \tag{2.26}$$

where $r = (r_1, \ldots, r_J)$ is the price vector for the undesirable outputs.

Since $R(x,p,r) \geqq py - ru$ for all feasible $(y, u) \in P(x)$ and $(y + \vec{D}_o(x, y, u; g_y, g_u)g_y, u - \vec{D}_o(x, y, u; g_y.g_u)g_u)$ is feasible, we have

$$\frac{R(x,p,r) - (py - ru)}{pg_y + rg_u} \geqq \vec{D}_o(x, y, u; g_y, g_u). \tag{2.27}$$

One may show that if the output set is a closed, nonempty convex set then the output distance function $\vec{D}_o(x, y, u; g_y, g_u)$ can be retrieved from the revenue function as

$$\vec{D}_o(x, y, u; g_y, g_u) = \inf_{p,r} \frac{R(x,p,r) - (py - ru)}{pg_y + rg_u}. \tag{2.28}$$

If the distance function is differentiable, then the envelope theorem yields the following shadow prices

$$\nabla_y \vec{D}_o(x, y, u; g_y, g_u) = \frac{-p}{pg_y + rg_u} \tag{2.29}$$

and

$$\nabla_u \vec{D}_o(x, y, u; g_y, g_u) = \frac{r}{pg_y + rg_u}. \tag{2.30}$$

Both sets of shadow prices are normalized by the value of the directional vector. If we assume that one price is known, for example one of the prices of the desirable outputs, then we may compute the absolute price for the undesirable output. If we assume that p_m is known (and equal to its shadow price) then by the conditions for the two sets of shadow prices above, we may compute the price of the j'th bad output as

$$r_j = -p_m \frac{\frac{\partial \vec{D}_o}{\partial u_j}(x, y, u; g_y, g_u)}{\frac{\partial \vec{D}_o}{\partial y_m}(x, y, u; g_y, g_u)}. \tag{2.31}$$

The above expression shows that the shadow prices depend on the directional vector $g = (g_y, g_u)$. However if two vectors are proportional, i.e., $g' = \lambda g^o, \lambda \in \Re$ or $\vec{D}_o(x,y,u;g') = \vec{D}_o(x,y,u;g^o) = 0$, then the shadow price is independent of this vector.

To see this recall that if the output set is convex, closed and nonempty, then any boundary point has a supporting hyperplane. Thus the relative prices for this output vector are given. Define two boundary points for g' and g^o, where $v = (y,u)$ and $g = (g_y, g_u)$ as

$$\hat{v}' = v + \vec{D}_o(x,y,u;g')g'$$

and

$$\hat{v}^o = v + \vec{D}_o(x,y,u;g^o)g^o.$$

If $\vec{D}_o(x,y,u;g') = \vec{D}_o(x,y,u;g^o) = 0$ then it follows that $\hat{v}' = \hat{v}^o$, and therefore these have the same shadow price vector.

If the direction vectors are proportional, $g' = \lambda g^o$, then it follows that

$$\begin{aligned} \hat{v}' &= v + \vec{D}_o(x,y,u;\lambda g^o)\lambda g^o \\ &= v + \vec{D}_o(x,y,u;g^o)g^o = \hat{v}^o, \end{aligned} \tag{2.32}$$

since the directional distance function is homogeneous of degree -1 in the directional vector. Thus in the cases above the shadow prices are independent of the directional vector.

Conversely if $\hat{v}' = \hat{v}^o$, then it follows that

$$\vec{D}_o(x,y,u;g')g'_m = \vec{D}_o(x,y,u;g^o)g^o_m$$

or

$$\vec{D}_o(x,y,u;g') = \vec{D}_o(x,y,u;g^o)g^o_m/g'_m, \text{ for all m,}$$

where g_m is the m'th component of the vector.
Thus

$$g' = \lambda g^o, \lambda \in \Re$$

or

$$\vec{D}_o(x,y,u;g') = \vec{D}_o(x,y,u;g^o).$$

This shows that if there are no flat spots on the isoquant of the output set, then the above are the only cases for which the shadow prices are independent of the directional vector.

To translate the shadow price formula (2.31) into empirical results requires that we parameterize the distance function. Recall that the directional distance function satisfies the translation property, i.e,

$$\vec{D}_o(x, y + \alpha g_y, u - \alpha g_u; g_y, g_u) = \vec{D}_o(x, y, u; g_y, g_u) - \alpha. \tag{2.33}$$

As it turns out, the quadratic function is a parametric function that can be easily restricted to satisfy the translation property. In contrast, the translog function can readily be restricted to satisfy homogeneity, but not translation. If we let $g_y = 1$ and $g_u = -1$, we have

$$\begin{aligned} \vec{D}_o(x, y, u; 1, 1) &= \alpha_o + \sum_{n=1}^{N} \alpha_n x_n + \sum_{m=1}^{M} \beta_m y_m \\ &+ \sum_{j=1}^{J} \gamma_j u_j + (1/2) \sum_{n=1}^{N} \sum_{n'=1}^{N} \alpha_{nn'} x_n x_{n'} \\ &+ (1/2) \sum_{m=1}^{M} \sum_{m'=1}^{M} \beta_{mm'} y_m y_{m'} \\ &+ (1/2) \sum_{j=1}^{J} \sum_{j'=1}^{J} \gamma_{jj'} u_j u_{j'} + \sum_{n=1}^{N} \sum_{m=1}^{M} \delta_{nm} x_n y_m \\ &+ \sum_{n=1}^{N} \sum_{j=1}^{J} \nu_{nj} x_n u_j + \sum_{m=1}^{M} \sum_{j=1}^{J} \mu_{mj} y_m u_j. \end{aligned} \tag{2.34}$$

Rather than giving general conditions for this function to satisfy the translation condition, we look at a simple example with one input, one good output and one bad output. In this case translation implies that we have

$$\begin{aligned} &\alpha_o + \alpha_1 x + \beta_1 (y + \alpha) + \gamma_1 (u - \alpha) + (1/2)\alpha_2 x^2 \\ &+(1/2)\beta_2 (y + \alpha)^2 + (1/2)\gamma_2 (u - \alpha)^2 + \delta x (y + \alpha) \\ &+\nu x (u - \alpha) + \mu (y + \alpha)(u - \alpha) \quad = \\ &\alpha_o + \alpha_1 x_1 + \beta_1 y + \gamma_1 u + (1/2)\alpha_2 x^2 + (1/2)\beta_2 y^2 \\ &+(1/2)\gamma_2 u^2 + \delta x y + +\nu x u + \mu y u - \alpha \end{aligned} \tag{2.35}$$

This expression implies that the parameters should be restricted as:

$$\beta_1 - \gamma_1 = 1, \beta_2 = \gamma_2 = \mu, \delta - \nu = 0.$$

Following this procedure one may estimate the parameter conditions for any empirical situation.

We may estimate our quadratic directional distance function using either linear programming methods following Aigner and Chu (1968) or as a stochastic frontier model. In the Aigner and Chu framework, we estimate the parameters of the distance function (2.34) so that it solves the following linear programming problem

$$\min \sum_{k=1}^{K} (\vec{D}_o(x^k, y^k, u^k; 1, 1) - 0)$$

subject to:

(i) $\vec{D}_o(x^k, y^k, u^k; 1, 1) \geqq 0, k = 1, \ldots, K,$

(ii) $\frac{\partial \vec{D}_o(x^k, y^k, u^k; 1,1)}{\partial u_j} \geqq 0, k = 1, \ldots, K, j = 1, \ldots, J,$

(iii) $\frac{\partial \vec{D}_o(x^k, y^k, u^k; 1,1)}{\partial y_m} \leqq 0, k = 1, \ldots, K, m = 1, \ldots, M,$

(iv) $\frac{\partial \vec{D}_o(x^k, y^k, u^k; 1,1)}{\partial x_n} \geqq 0, k = 1, \ldots, K, n = 1, \ldots, N$

(v) conditions for translation property,

(vi) symmetry.

Condition (i) imposes feasibility, establishing the distance function as a frontier while (ii), (iii) and (iv) are monotonicity requirements. Finally (v) imposes the translation property for the case in which technology is specified as quadratic. One may retrieve the normalized shadow prices of the undesirable outputs by applying the envelope property in (2.30) and substituting the estimated parameter values from the programming problem above; these may be retrieved directly from the restrictions in (ii). Nonnormalized shadow prices can then be estimated using (2.31), i.e., by taking the ratio of the derivative of bad to good output multiplied by the negative of the price of the desirable output chosen as numeraire.

In the next two sections we include applications of our environmental models. The first provides an example of how the relationship between property rights and profitability may be addressed using our environmental models. The second is an empirical application of our index number approach.

5. Property Rights and Profitability

by

R. Färe, S. Grosskopf and W.-F. Lee

The absence of property rights has long been recognized as a source of market failure. Examples include the case of externalities and common-pool resources. Coase (1960) proposed the creation and enforcement of property rights as a solution to the externality problem. Property rights serve the same purpose in preventing the tragedy of the commons. While property rights are a means of achieving a Pareto efficient allocation, the effect on the distribution of income (or profitability) depends on who receives the property rights. The purpose of this paper is to investigate the relationship between property rights and profitability using DEA (Data Envelopment Analysis)[3] and the network theory of production, i.e., Network DEA.

In this section we consider the effect of property rights on profitability in the presence of externalities and in the presence of a common-pool resource. In the former, we confine our attention to the case of a negative externality in which an upstream agent produces good and bad outputs (a paper and pulp mill for example), and the bad outputs adversely affect the downstream agent's production opportunity (a fishery for example). The common-pool resource we have in mind is the classic case of fishing grounds.

The next section sets up the production technology we use in both cases based on a DEA model and network theory. Next we address the effects of assignment of property rights on profitability in the presence of the externality. Three cases are considered: 1) the upstream agent has the property right, 2) the downstream agent has the property right, and 3) the externality is internalized to a network. Comparing the individual profits under the three regimes provides an estimate of the redistribution associated with the assignment of property rights as well as providing for an upper bound on transaction costs. We also include the case of a common-pool resource. Here we set up a model which solves for op-

[3]This expression was coined by Charnes, Cooper and Rhodes (1978).

timal individual quotas (property rights) in the presence of a common pool resource with restrictions ensuring preservation of the fish stock for future periods.

5.1 The Production Network with Externality

In this paper we take a network approach (see Färe, 1991 or Färe and Grosskopf, 1996) to modeling the interaction between agents in the presence of externalities and common-pool resources. We begin with the case of the externality and then turn to the common-pool resource case.

We begin with the case of one polluter and one receptor, a restriction that may be relaxed. To illustrate the interaction we assume that there are two technologies, represented by their output sets P^1 and P^2. These sets and their interactions are illustrated in Figure 2.3.

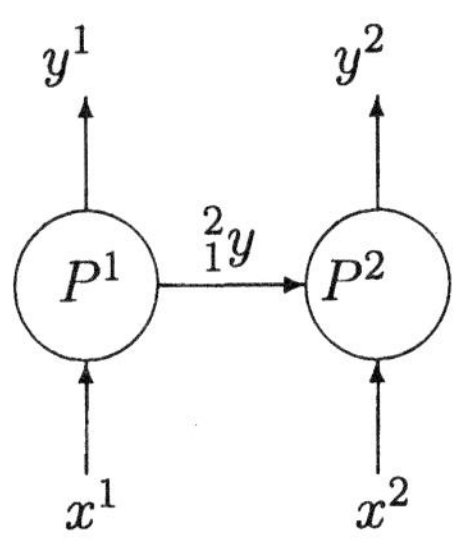

Figure 2.3. The Network Model with Externality

The upstream technology, P^1 uses input vector $x^1 \in \Re^N_+$ to produce two sets of outputs. The first set $y^1 \in \Re^M_+$ denotes final products that are traded on the market (for example, paper), and the second set ${}^2_1y \in \Re^J_+$ are those outputs that are used as inputs in the second technology, and that are potentially detrimental to this technology (for example, polluted water). Here we use ${}^2_1y$ as our notation for this externality; it can be either positive or negative. These two sets of outputs are produced jointly by the upstream firm. Here we use the terminology of joint production in the sense of Shephard and Färe (1974) and say that y^1 is null-joint with ${}_1^2y$ if $(y^1, {}_1^2y) \in P(x^1)$ and ${}_1^2y = 0$ imply that $y^1 = 0$. Null-jointness thus implies that positive final outputs $y^1 \geqq 0, y^1 \neq 0$ can only be produced if some bad output ${}_1^2y$ is also produced.

The outputs ${}_1^2y$ are assumed to be pollutants, which have a negative impact on the downstream technology $P^2(x^2, {}_1^2y)$. The downstream technology (the fishery) cannot avoid using the ${}_1^2y$ as an input, and we assume that all outputs ${}_1^2y$ from the upstream firm are inputs to the fishery. This assumption may be relaxed.

To model the unfavorable impact of ${}_1^2y$ on the downstream firm, we assume that this technology exhibits weak disposability of inputs, i.e.,

$$P^2(\lambda x^2, \lambda {}_1^2y) \supseteq P^2(x^2, {}_1^2y), \lambda \geqq 1 \tag{2.36}$$

and that ${}_1^2y$ are congesting in the sense that

$$P^2(x^2, {}_1^2y) \supseteq P^2(x^2, {}_1^2y'), \text{ if } {}_1^2y' \geqq {}_1^2y. \tag{2.37}$$

In words, (2.36) says that if all inputs are increased proportionally, then output does not decrease, while (2.37) expresses the idea that if bad inputs ${}_1^2y$ are increased output y^2 does not increase–it may even decrease.

The network model illustrated in Figure 2.3 may be formalized as two interacting activity analysis or DEA models. To see this we assume for simplicity that there are $k = 1, \ldots, K$ observations of each of the two technologies; an assumption which may be generalized to different numbers of observations for each technology. We start by modeling the upstream technology.

$$\begin{aligned} P^1(x^1) &= \{(y^1, {}_1^2y) &:& \quad (2.38)\\ \delta\, y_m^1 &\leqq \sum_{k=1}^{K} z_k^1 y_{km}^1, m = 1, \ldots, M, \\ \delta\, {}_1^2y_j &= \sum_{k=1}^{K} z_k^1\, {}_1^2y_{kj}, j = 1, \ldots, J, \\ x_n^1 &\geqq \sum_{k=1}^{K} z_k^1 x_{kn}^1, n = 1, \ldots, N, \end{aligned}$$

$$
\begin{aligned}
z_k^1 &\geqq 0, k = 1, \ldots, K, \\
\sum_{k=1}^{K} z_k^1 &\leq 1, \\
\delta &\geqq 1\}.
\end{aligned}
$$

Here the observations (data) are y_{km}^1, ${}_1^2y_{kj}$ and x_{kn}^1; they denote the kth observation of final output m, intermediate or 'bad' output j (which is an input into the second technology), and direct input n, respectively.

The upstream technology in (2.38) satisfies nonincreasing returns to scale due to the restriction on the intensity variables $z_k^1, k = \ldots, K$, which implies nonnegative profit. The outputs $(y^1, {}_1^2y)$ are weakly disposable in the sense that

$$
\text{if } (y^1, {}_1^2y) \in P^1(x^1) \text{ and } 0 \leqq \theta \leqq 1 \text{ then } (\theta y^1, \theta\, {}_1^2y) \in P^1(x^1). \tag{2.39}
$$

Note that in (2.38), a scalar δ has been added to the final output and intermediate output constraints. This is required for the technology to satisfy weak disposability in the absence of constant returns to scale. In the case in which the upstream firm has no constraints on disposal of the intermediate output (for example, if the upstream firm has the property right), then the problem could be specified without the delta parameter and with an inequality in the intermediate output constraints.
In addition the final outputs y^1 are freely disposable. This condition follows from inequality in the first M constraints. Finally inputs x^1 are freely disposable, i.e.,

$$
x^1 \geqq \hat{x}^1 \text{ implies that } P^1(x^1) \supseteq P^1(\hat{x}^1). \tag{2.40}
$$

To model the downstream technology P^2, we assume again that there are $k = 1, \ldots, K$ observations of inputs $(x_{kn}^2, {}_1^2y_{kj})$ and outputs y_{km}^2. The DEA model of the downstream technology may be written as

$$
\begin{aligned}
P^2(x^2, {}_1^2y) &= \{y^2 \quad : \quad && (2.41)\\
y_m^2 &\leqq \sum_{k=1}^{K} z_k^2 y_{km}^2, m = 1, \ldots, M, \\
\gamma\, {}_1^2y_j &= \sum_{k=1}^{K} z_k^2\, {}_1^2y_{kj}, j = 1, \ldots, J,
\end{aligned}
$$

$$\begin{aligned} \gamma\, x_n^2 &\geqq \sum_{k=1}^{K} z_k^2 x_{kn}^2, n = 1, \ldots, N, \\ z_k^2 &\geqq 0, k = 1, \ldots, K, \\ \sum_{k=1}^{K} z_k^2 &\leqq 1, 0 \leqq \gamma \leqq 1\}. \end{aligned}$$

Outputs y_m^2 and inputs x_n^2 are freely disposable as seen by the corresponding inequalities in their constraints. The downstream technology satisfies weak disposability of inputs (including the upstream intermediate outputs), due to the inclusion of the scaling factor γ.

Up to this point, the upstream and downstream technologies have been modeled independently (the downstream firm treats the 'bad' inputs as exogenous). Next we integrate them into a network. Network output is equal to the sum of the two internalized technologies' outputs. We note that the final output vectors of both technologies belong to $\Re_+^M$. This does not imply, however, that they need to produce the same outputs; some components of the output vector may be zero.[4]

The network exogenous (total) input is x which is at least as large as $x^1 + x^2$. The vector ${}_1^2y$ now becomes an intermediate product; it is produced and used within the network. Under these conditions our network technology may be written

$$\begin{aligned} P(x) = \quad \{y : \; & y = y^1 + y^2 \\ & (y^1, {}_1^2y) \in P^1(x^1) \\ & y^2 \in P^2(x^2, {}_1^2y) \\ & x^1 + x^2 \leqq x\}. \end{aligned} \tag{2.42}$$

One can prove that in this model, inputs $(x_1, \ldots, x_N)$ and outputs $(y_1, \ldots, y_M)$ are freely disposable and that the network technology satisfies nonincreasing returns to scale in the sense that

$$P(\lambda x) \supseteq \lambda P(x), \lambda \geqq 1. \tag{2.43}$$

[4]For our example, the entire output vector includes both paper and fish. The upstream firm produces zero fish and the downstream firm produces zero paper.

Disposability follows from the inequalities in (2.41) plus the corresponding inequalities in (2.38). Nonincreasing returns to scale is a consequence of the restrictions on the intensity variables z_k^1 and $z_k^2, k = 1, \ldots, K.$,

5.2 Common-pool Resource Technology

Here we model the case of $k = 1, \ldots, K$ firms (or fishing vessels) which employ inputs $x_n, n = 1, \ldots, N$ to 'produce' outputs $y_m, m = 1, \ldots, M$. In the absence of regulation the static one period technology may be represented simply as

$$
\begin{aligned}
P(x^{k'}) = \{y : \quad y_m &\leqq \textstyle\sum_{k=1}^K z_k y_{km}, \quad m = 1, \ldots, M, \\
x_n^{k'} &\geqq \textstyle\sum_{k=1}^K z_k x_{kn}, \quad n = 1, \ldots, N, \\
z_k &\geqq 0, \quad k = 1, \ldots, K, \\
\textstyle\sum_{k=1}^K z_k &\leqq 1\}.
\end{aligned} \tag{2.44}
$$

This specification of the technology does not explicitly account for the fact that each individual firm is competing for a share of the fixed (in the short run) total fishing stock. One could introduce a constraint much like that associated with the 'bad' output in our externality model, to capture the 'congesting' effects of the other firms. However, modeling technology as a network allows us to include the common-pool resource aspect even more directly. Let B_m represent the 'biomass' or stock of resource (or fish type) $m = 1, \ldots, M$. Then in the network, the sum of the individual outputs cannot exceed this bound, i.e., we have

$$
\begin{aligned}
P(x) = \quad \{y : \quad & B_m \geqq \sum_{k=1}^K y_{km}, m = 1, \ldots, M \\
& y^k \in P^k(x^k) \\
& \sum_{k=1}^K x^k \leqq x\}.
\end{aligned} \tag{2.45}
$$

One can introduce limits on reduction of the biomass by changing the network constraint to $\lambda B_m \geqq \sum_{k=1}^K y_{km}, m = 1, \ldots, M$, where $\lambda < 1$ and may be determined by biological considerations.

5.3 Property Rights, Profit and Externalities

In this section we develop profit maximization models for our externality and common-pool resource problems. We begin with our externality model. We consider three cases: 1) the upstream firm is given the property right to the 'stream', 2) the downstream firm is given the property right, and 3) the property right is internalized into the network. In each case we are interested in the distribution of profits of the individual firms.

We model the case in which the upstream polluter has the property right to the stream by allowing the upstream firm to maximize profit with no constraints on the production of bad outputs ${}_1^2y$. The solution yields profit and the 'optimal' ${}_1^2y*$. This output vector is then taken as exogenous input for the downstream firm, which in the next step maximizes its profit given ${}_1^2y*$. Formally, given output prices $p \in \Re_+^M$ and input prices $w \in \Re_+^N$, the upstream firm's profit maximization problem is

$$
\begin{aligned}
\Pi^1(p,w) = \quad & \max_{y^1,{}_1^2y,x^1} \sum_{m=1}^{M} p_m y_m^1 - \sum_{n=1}^{N} w_n x_n^1 && (2.46)\\
\text{s.t.} \quad & \delta\, y_m^1 \leqq \sum_{k=1}^{K} z_k^1 y_{km}^1, m = 1,\ldots,M, \\
& \delta\, {}_1^2y_j = \sum_{k=1}^{K} z_k^1\, {}_1^2y_{kj}, j = 1,\ldots,J, \\
& x_n^1 \geqq \sum_{k=1}^{K} z_k^1 x_{kn}^1, n = 1,\ldots,N, \\
& z_k^1 \geqq 0, k = 1,\ldots,K, \\
& \sum_{k=1}^{K} z_k^1 \leqq 1, \delta \geqq 1.
\end{aligned}
$$

The solution to this problem gives the maximal profit when the upstream firm has the property right. The solution also yields a vector of optimal bad outputs ${}_1^2y_j^*, j = 1,\ldots,J$. Taking this as given for the downstream firm, we can estimate the downstream firm's profit as

$$
\Pi^2(p,w,{}_1^2y^*) = \max_{y^2,x^2} \sum_{m=1}^{M} p_m y_m^2 - \sum_{n=1}^{N} w_n x_n^2 \qquad (2.47)
$$

$$\begin{aligned}
\text{s.t.} \quad y_m^2 &\leqq \sum_{k=1}^{K} z_k^2 y_{km}^2, m = 1, \ldots, M, \\
\gamma\, {}_1^2y_j^* &= \sum_{k=1}^{K} z_k^2\, {}_1^2y_{kj}, j = 1, \ldots, J, \\
\gamma x_n^2 &\geqq \sum_{k=1}^{K} z_k^2 x_{kn}^2, n = 1, \ldots, N, \\
z_k^2 &\geqq 0, k = 1, \ldots, K, \\
\sum_{k=1}^{K} z_k^2 &\leqq 1, 0 \leqq \gamma \leqq 1.
\end{aligned}$$

Before turning to our second case, a few remarks are in order. If there is no regulation and no property right is granted we might expect the problems above to yield a likely outcome, i.e., these could serve as a model for the unregulated case. The fact that the upstream firm is assumed to be given the property right (i.e., the right to pollute), does not, in this model, necessarily lead to the Coase efficient outcome, since there are no side payments included in the model. However, we could use these two problems to compute the loss in profit to the upstream firm and gain in profit to the downstream firm of reducing emissions below ${}_1^2y^*$.[5]

Turning to our second case, if we grant the property right to the downstream firm we have a second pair of profit maximization problems. Now we solve the downstream firm's problem first, i.e.,

$$\Pi^2(p, w) = \max_{y^2, {}_1^2y, x^2} \sum_{m=1}^{M} p_m y_m^2 - \sum_{n=1}^{N} w_n x_n^2 \tag{2.48}$$

$$\begin{aligned}
\text{s.t.} \quad y_m^2 &\leqq \sum_{k=1}^{K} z_k^2 y_{km}^2, m = 1, \ldots, M, \\
\gamma\, {}_1^2y_j &= \sum_{k=1}^{K} z_k^2\, {}_1^2y_{kj}, j = 1, \ldots, J, \\
\gamma x_n^2 &\geqq \sum_{k=1}^{K} z_k^2 x_{kn}^2, n = 1, \ldots, N,
\end{aligned}$$

[5]In principle, by reducing ${}_1^2y^*$ to zero, we would have the case in which the downstream firm would in effect have the property right.

$$z_k^2 \geqq 0, k = 1, \ldots, K,$$
$$\sum_{k=1}^{K} z_k^2 \leqq 1, 0 \leqq \gamma \leqq 1.$$

In addition to obtaining the maximal profit for the downstream firm when they have the property right, this expression yields a vector of optimal inputs ${}_1^2y_j^{**}, j = 1, \ldots, J$. Note that we might expect the downstream firm to choose ${}_1^2y_j^{**}, j = 1, \ldots, J$ to be zero, since they are undesirable from the viewpoint of the downstream firm. However, without data, one could not exclude the possibility of positive ${}_1^2y$ from consideration. These inputs are outputs from the viewpoint of the upstream firm, and therefore become parameters in the upstream firm's problem when the downstream firm has the property right. Thus for the upstream firm we have

$$\begin{aligned}
\Pi^1(p, w, {}_1^2y^{**}) = \quad & \max_{y^1, x^1} \sum_{m=1}^{M} p_m y_m^1 - \sum_{n=1}^{N} w_n x_n^1 & (2.49)\\
\text{s.t.} \quad & \delta\, y_m^1 \leqq \sum_{k=1}^{K} z_k^1 y_{km}^1, m = 1, \ldots, M, \\
& \delta\, {}_1^2y_j^{**} = \sum_{k=1}^{K} z_k^1\, {}_1^2y_{kj}, j = 1, \ldots, J, \\
& x_n^1 \geqq \sum_{k=1}^{K} z_k^1 x_{kn}^1, n = 1, \ldots, N, \\
& z_k^1 \geqq 0, k = 1, \ldots, K, \\
& \sum_{k=1}^{K} z_k^1 \leqq 1, \delta \geqq 1.
\end{aligned}$$

Again, this solution does not account for potential bargaining à la Coase. Comparisons of (2.46) and (2.49) for the upstream firm and (2.47) and (2.48) for the downstream firm would, however, give an estimate of the maximum potential redistribution of 'income' that changes in the assignment of property rights entail. Clearly, we would expect firm profit to be higher if the firm has the property right. Taking the difference in profits for each firm with and without property rights would give an estimate of potential 'rents' to be gained.[6]

Our final profit maximization problem with externalities deals with the situation when the externalities ${}^2_1y_i, i = 1, \ldots, I$ are internalized. This corresponds to maximization of profit with the network technology as constraints. In this case we have

$$
\begin{aligned}
\Pi(p, w,) = \quad \max_{y^1, y^2, {}^2_1y, x} \quad & \sum_{m=1}^{M} p_m y_m - \sum_{n=1}^{N} w_n x_n \qquad (2.50)\\
\text{s.t.} \quad & y_m = y^1_m + y^2_m, m = 1, \ldots, M \\
& \delta\, y^1_m \leqq \sum_{k=1}^{K} z^1_k y^1_{km}, m = 1, \ldots, M, \\
& \delta\, {}^2_1y_j = \sum_{k=1}^{K} z^1_k\, {}^2_1y_{kj}, j = 1, \ldots, J, \\
& x^1_n \geqq \sum_{k=1}^{K} z^1_k x^1_{kn}, n = 1, \ldots, N, \\
& z^1_k \geqq 0, k = 1, \ldots, K, \\
& \sum_{k=1}^{K} z^1_k \leq 1, \delta \geqq 1, \\
& y^2_m \leqq \sum_{k=1}^{K} z^2_k y^2_{km}, m = 1, \ldots, M, \\
& \gamma\, {}^2_1y_j = \sum_{k=1}^{K} z^2_k\, {}^2_1y_{kj}, j = 1, \ldots, J, \\
& \gamma\, x^2_n \geqq \sum_{k=1}^{K} z^2_k x^2_{kn}, n = 1, \ldots, N, \\
& z^2_k \geqq 0, k = 1, \ldots, K, \\
& \sum_{k=1}^{K} z^2_k \leqq 1, 0 \leqq \gamma \leqq 1, \\
& x^1_n + x^2_n \leq x_n, n = 1, \ldots, N
\end{aligned}
$$

[6]As suggested to us by Quentin Grafton, one could also use these estimates as bounds on potential transactions costs to determine the feasibility of a Coase solution.

In principle, these problems are very simple to compute if the relevant data are available. Despite their simplicity, they explicitly model the key aspects involved in production externalities: 1) the joint production of good and bad outputs, 2) the role of bads as an 'intermediate' input which adversely affects production of other firms, and 3) the potential lack of free disposability of bads. Formulation of these problems in a profit maximization framework allows us to simulate the redistribution of 'income' which would result from a change in ownership of property rights as well as allowing us to solve for the efficient outcome under merger or internalization of the externality.

Some remarks concerning the network model: 1) the network output vector is not necessarily greater than the sum of the two independent technologies' output vectors, and 2) the network profits are at least equal to the sum of the two independent technologies' profits. Thus we can measure the gain in potential profit from internalization of the externality, which could be used as a compensation benchmark for the agents involved when considering merger or buy out. Alternatively, one could use the solution vector from the network problem to set optimal quantity constraints for the effluents or to verify whether existing restrictions are optimal.[7]

5.4 Property rights, profits and a common-pool resource

Next we model profit maximization in our common-pool resource case. In the absence of coordination or regulation in the industry, firms would maximize profits (in the short-run single period case) by solving the following problem

$$\begin{aligned} \Pi^{k'}(p,w) = \quad & \max_{y^{k'},x^{k'}} \sum_{m=1}^{M} p_m y_m^{k'} - \sum_{n=1}^{N} w_n x_n^{k'} \qquad (2.51) \\ \text{s.t.} \quad & y_m^{k'} \leqq \sum_{k=1}^{K} z_k y_{km}, m = 1, \ldots, M, \end{aligned}$$

[7] Brännlund, Färe and Grosskopf (1995) use a similar activity analysis model to compute the loss in of profits due to regulatory constraints restricting emissions in the paper and pulp industry in Sweden. Brännlund, Chung, Färe and Grosskopf (1998) modify that model to simulate emissions trading in the same industry.

$$
\begin{aligned}
x_n^{k'} &\geq \sum_{k=1}^{K} z_k x_{kn}, n = 1, \ldots, N, \\
z_k &\geqq 0, k = 1, \ldots, K, \\
\sum_{k=1}^{K} z_k &\leqq 1.
\end{aligned}
$$

Given the common-pool resource, the solution to this problem could well yield an inefficient allocation from a social long-term viewpoint. Again, we can use a network to model an optimal solution to this problem. Specifically,

$$
\begin{aligned}
\Pi(p, w) = \quad & \max_{y,x} \sum_{m=1}^{M} p_m y_m - \sum_{n=1}^{N} w_n x_n && (2.52) \\
\text{s.t.} \quad & \lambda_m B_m \geq \sum_{k'=1}^{K} y_m^{k'} (= y_m), m = 1, \ldots, M \\
& y_m^{k'} \leqq \sum_{k=1}^{K} z_k^{k'} y_{km}, m = 1, \ldots, M; k' = 1, \ldots, K \\
& x_n^{k'} \geqq \sum_{k=1}^{K} z_k^{k'} x_{kn}, n = 1, \ldots, N; k' = 1, \ldots, K \\
& z_k^{k'} \geqq 0, k = 1, \ldots, K, k' = 1, \ldots, K, \\
& \sum_{k=1}^{K} z_k^{k'} \leqq 1, k' = 1, \ldots, K, \\
& \sum_{k'=1}^{K} x_n^{k'} \leqq x_n, n = 1, \ldots, N.
\end{aligned}
$$

This is a very large problem–there are a set of intensity variables for each firm (the index over k'), as well as a set of input and output constraints for each firm, again indexed over k'. In turn there are constraints that put bounds on input use and fish catch for the network as a whole (the first and last constraints). The solution to this problem gives industry profits as well as the optimal 'catch' for each type of fish for each 'firm'. This could be used to assign a property right (individual quota) for each firm. This problem will assign larger 'quotas' to more efficient firms (since that will maximize group profit). Nevertheless, by including variables that reflect boat size, type, etc in the vector of inputs, one can 'customize' these quotas. That entails including these capital restrictions as 'fixed' rather than variable inputs, as in Brännlund *et al* (1998).

Clearly, this is a very simplified version of the common-pool resource problem. One should, of course, include dynamics in the model. In principle, this is not difficult in a network model, and has the advantages of being readily computable using discrete time data. For an example, see Chambers, Färe and Grosskopf (1996) or Färe and Whittaker (1996). A perhaps more difficult problem is the introduction of uncertainty into the problem.

5.5 Summary

The goal of this section is to specify computable models that can be used to investigate the effect of assignment of property rights on profitability in the presence of sources of market failure. The cases we consider are a simple production externality and a common-pool resource. In modeling the production externality we specifically include joint production of goods and bads and the explicit deleterious effects of the jointly produced bad on the downstream firm. One of the innovations is to show how to use a network model to solve for the efficient allocation of resources in the presence of an externality. By employing a profit maximization model, we can solve for optimal emissions as well as providing estimates of rents and bounds on transactions costs, for example.

In the common-pool resource problem, we use a network model again to model the group problem of allocating resources in the absence of property rights. By computing a network profit maximization problem for the group of firms 'sharing' the common-pool resource we can solve for optimal individual quotas. The model developed here is a static model with a fixed bound on the biomass involved. Clearly the next step is to generalize this to a dynamic network model.

6. An Environmental Kuznets Curve for the OECD Countries

by

Rolf Färe, Shawna Grosskopf and Osman Zaim

Since Grossman and Krueger's (1991) path breaking study which shows that an inverted U-type relationship exists between the level of emissions and per capita income (i.e., Environmental Kuznets Curve), a large literature has emerged estimating Environmental Kuznets Curves and their implications. To show the existence (or non-existence) of an Environmental Kuznets Curve, the typical approach has been to estimate either quadratic or polynomial functional forms to estimate the statistical relation between simple, individual measures of environmental performance, such as emissions and per capita income (together with some control variables). For example, changes in SO_2, dark matter (fine smoke) and suspended particles (SPM) in Grossman and Krueger (1991), total annual deforestation and nine different environmental indicators[8] in Shafik and Bandyopadhyay (1992), four different air borne emissions (SO_2, NO_x, SPM and CO) in Selden and Song, (1994), the rate of deforestation in Cropper and Griffith (1994) and carbon dioxide per capita in Holtz-Eakin and Selden (1995) are all related to per capita income and various control variables. These results empirically support the existence of an environmental Kuznets curve for air pollutants such as suspended particulate matter, sulfur dioxide and NO_x. While for the water pollutants the results are mixed, for the specific air pollutant CO_2, the relationship has been found to be monotonically increasing with per capita incomes, i.e., there is no Kuznets curve for CO_2.

Common to all these studies is a reduced form approach which typically ignores the underlying production process which converts inputs into outputs and pollutants, while in fact it is the modification or transformation of the production process that may lead to improved environmental performance at higher income levels. Furthermore, the fact that these studies analyze the relationship between environmental performance and growth for each of the many pollutants individually, i.e., in a partial equilibrium framework, implies that a clear-cut policy conclusion is very unlikely.

The obvious need for a single environmental performance index and a method which implicitly recognizes the underlying production process which transforms inputs into outputs and pollutants gave rise to a number of studies which focus on production theory in measuring environmental performance. These studies, by exploiting the aggregator characteristics of distance functions, derived various indexes which measure the environmental efficiency of various producing units. For example Färe, Grosskopf and Pasurka (1989), by using radial measures of techni-

[8]The nine other indicators are lack of clean water, lack of urban sanitation, ambient levels of suspended particulate matter, ambient sulfur oxides, change in forest area between 1961 and 1986, dissolved oxygen in rivers, fecal coliforms in rivers, municipal waste per capita and carbon emissions per capita.

cal efficiency, compute the opportunity cost of transforming a technology from one where production units costlessly release environmentally hazardous substances, to one in which it is costly to release. In another study, Färe, Grosskopf, Lovell and Pasurka (1989) suggested an hyperbolic measure of efficiency (which allows for simultaneous equiproportionate reduction in the undesirable output and expansion in the desirable outputs[9] in measuring the opportunity cost of such transformation. Finally Zaim and Taskin (2000) and Taskin and Zaim (2000) by applying these techniques to macro level data provided evidence for the existence of a Kuznets type relationship between measures of environmental efficiency and per capita income level.

In a more recent study, Färe, Grosskopf and Hernandez-Sancho (forthcoming) propose an alternative index number approach to environmental performance which measures the degree to which a plant or a firm succeeds in expanding its good outputs while simultaneously accounting for bad outputs. The proposed index consists of the ratio of the quantity index of good outputs to a quantity index of bad outputs, the implicit benchmark being the highest ratio of good to bad outputs. In this study we first explore the environmental performance of the OECD countries between 1971-1990 and then examine the existence of a Kuznets type relationship between income and environmental performance as measured by this new index. Thus we provide a means of simultaneously accounting for multiple pollutants within a production theoretic framework that is at once rigorous (based on axiomatic production theory) yet unrestrictive—our empirical technique imposes no functional form on the underlying technology. In fact we use distance functions, natural aggregator functions as our building blocks, which yield index numbers consistent with the properties laid out by Fisher (1922).

The next section will introduce the methodology followed by the presentation of the data source and discussion of results.

6.1 Methodology

In this section we describe the environmental index adopted here.[10] In short, the index is defined as the ratio of a good output quantity index and a quantity index of bad or undesirable outputs. Each of the two

[9]Here various measures of environmental performance are proposed depending on whether reductions in inputs together with undesirable outputs are sought.

[10]For a survey of environmental performance indexes, not including the one adopted here, see Tyteca(1996).

indexes are based on distance functions, very much like the Malmquist (1953) index, but rather than scaling the full output vector, we scale good and bad outputs separately. Thus our index is developed using "sub-vector" distance functions.

To describe the environmental performance "index" some notation is needed. Assume that a vector of inputs $x = (x_1, \ldots, x_N) \in R_+^N$ produces a vector $y = (y_1, ..., y_M) \in R_+^M$ of good output and at the same time produces a vector $u = (u_1, ..., u_J) \in R_+^J$of bad outputs, then we define the production technology as

$$T = \{(x, y, u) : x \text{ can produce } (y, u)\}.$$

This technology producing both good and bad outputs is assumed to satisfy the following two conditions.

Weak disposability of outputs:
if $(x, y, u) \in T$ and $0 \leqq \theta \leqq 1$, $(x, \theta y, \theta u) \in T$

Null-jointness:
if $(x, y, u) \in T$ and $u = 0$ then $y = 0$.

Weak disposability models the following situation: reductions in outputs (y, u) are feasible, provided that they are proportional. This means proportional contraction of outputs can be made, but it may not be possible to reduce any single output by itself. In particular it may not be possible to freely dispose of a bad output.

The null-jointness condition tells us that for an input output vector (x, y, u) to be feasible with no bad output (u) produced, it is necessary that no good output (y) be produced. Put differently if good output is produced, some bad output is also produced. In addition to the above two properties on the technology T, we assume that it meets standard properties like closedness and convexity.

To formulate the good output quantity index, we define a subvector output distance function on the good outputs as

$$D_y(x, y, u) = \inf\{\theta : (x, y/\theta, u) \in T\}.$$

This distance function expands good outputs as much as is feasible, while keeping inputs and bad outputs fixed. Note that it is homogeneous of degree +1 in y. Let x^0 and u^0 be our given inputs and bad outputs, then the good output index compares two output vectors y^k and y^l.

This is done by taking the ratio of two distance functions, and hence, the good index is:

$$Q_y(x^0, u^0, y^k, y^l) = \frac{D_y(x^0, y^k, u^0)}{D_y(x^0, y^l, u^0)}.$$

This quantity index satisfies some of Fisher's (1922) important tests like homogeneity, time reversal, transitivity, and dimensionality.

The index of bad outputs is constructed using an "input" distance function approach. The argument is obvious, it is desirable to reduce such outputs. Thus the input based distance function is defined as

$$D_u(x, y, u) = \sup\{\lambda : (x, y, u/\lambda) \in T\}.$$

This distance function is homogeneous of degree +1 in bad outputs, and it is defined by finding the maximal contraction in these outputs. Given (x^0, y^0), the quantity index of bad outputs compares u^k and u^l again using the ratios of distance functions i.e.,

$$Q_u(x^0, y^0, u^k, u^l) = \frac{D_u(x^0, y^0, u^k)}{D_u(x^0, y^0, u^l)}.$$

Like the good index $Q_u(x^0, y^0, u^k, u^l)$ satisfies the above mentioned Fisher tests.

Next, following Färe, Grosskopf and Hernandez-Sancho (2004) we define the environmental performance index as the ratio of two quantity indexes, i.e.,

$$E^{k,l}(x^0, y^0, u^0, y^k, y^l, u^k, u^l) = \frac{Q_y(x^0, u^0, y^k, y^l)}{Q_u(x^0, y^0, u^k, u^l)}.$$

This performance index follows the tradition of Hicks-Moorsteen[11] by evaluating how much good output is produced per bad output.

In the simple case of one good and one bad output, the index takes the following simple form due to homogeneity of the component distance functions

$$E^{k,l} = \frac{y^k/u^k}{y^l/u^l}.$$

This one bad one good index shows that the index is the ratio of average good per bad output for k and l.

[11]See Diewert (1992) for references and terminology.

6.2 Data and Results

In computing the environmental performance indicators for each of the OECD countries in our sample, we chose aggregate output measured by Gross Domestic Product (GDP) expressed in international prices (1985 U.S. dollars) as the desirable output and carbon dioxide emissions (in metric tons) and solid particulate matter (in kilograms) as the two undesirable outputs. The two inputs considered are aggregate labor input as measured by total employment and total capital stock. The input and the desirable output data are compiled from the Penn World Tables (PWT 5,6) initially derived from the International Comparison Program benchmark where cross-country and over time comparisons are possible in real values.[12] Pollution related data are obtained from Monitoring Environmental Progress.[13]

In developing the environmental performance index, we used time series data for the years 1971-1990 for each of the OECD countries and constructed our index so that it compares each year in the sample with the initial year 1971 which then takes a value of unity.

In computing the distance functions, we chose the data envelopment analysis (DEA) (or activity analysis) methodology among competing alternatives, so as to take advantage of the fact that the distance functions are reciprocals of Farrell efficiency measures.

In this particular application, we chose the initial year 1971 as our reference. Thus we are assuming that $l = 0$ which then refers to the associated quantities for 1971. We let $k = 1, ..., K$ index the years in the sample. Thus for each year $k' = 1, ..., K$, we may estimate for each country

[12]The "Geary-Khamis" method that is used to obtain Purchasing Power Parities in the Penn World Tables has been questioned by Diewert (see for example Diewert (1999)) on grounds that this method may increase the relative share of a small country with respect to a larger one in multilateral comparisons. The computation of the environmental index that we will be discussing in the subsequent paragraphs in fact does not require an internationally comparable data (however, our analysis on Kuznets curve does). All it requires is GDP and capital stock expressed in domestic real currency (in addition to other physical inputs and bad outputs). Our trial runs of "good index" with OECD data where GDP is expressed in real currency units produced virtually identical results with those obtained from using Penn World Tables and hence proving the robustness of our indexes to the data set used. We thank Kevin Fox for bringing this point to our attention and simulating us to check or results with an alternative data set.

[13]The data can be reached from http://www.ciesin.org.

$$
\begin{aligned}
(D_y(x^0, y^{k'}, u^0))^{-1} &= \max \theta \qquad (2.53)\\
&st\\
\sum_{k=1}^{K} z_k y_m^k &\geq \theta y_m^{k'}, m = 1, ..., M,\\
\sum_{k=1}^{K} z_k u_j^k &= u_j^0, j = 1, ..., J,\\
\sum_{k=1}^{K} z_k x_n^k &\leq x_n^0, n = 1, ..., N,\\
z_k &\geq 0, k = 1, ..., K,
\end{aligned}
$$

which is the numerator for $Q_y(x^0, u^0, y^k, y^l)$. The denominator is computed by replacing $y^{k'}$ on the right hand side of the good output constraint with the observed output for the year 1971, i.e., y^0. This problem, using the observed data on desirable outputs, undesirable outputs and inputs between 1971 and 1990, constructs the best practice frontier for a particular country, and computes the scaling factor on good outputs required for each observation to attain best practice. The strict equality on the bad output constraints serves to impose weak disposability. Null-jointness holds provided that

$$
\begin{aligned}
\sum_{k=1}^{K} u_j^k &> 0, \; j = 1, \ldots, J\\
\sum_{j=1}^{J} u_j^k &> 0, \; k = 1, \ldots, K.
\end{aligned}
$$

The first condition states that each bad is produced at least once, and the last condition tells us that at each k some bad output is produced. All conditions are met for each country in our sample.

For the bad index, for a particular country, for each year $k' = 1, \ldots, K$ we compute

$$
(D_u(x^0, y^0, u^{k'}))^{-1} = \min \lambda
$$

$$
\begin{aligned}
& st \\
\sum_{k=1}^{K} z_k y_m^k &\geq y_m^0,\ m = 1, \ldots, M, \\
\sum_{k=1}^{K} z_k u_j^k &= \lambda u_j^{k'},\ j = 1, \ldots, J, \\
\sum_{k=1}^{K} z_k x_n^k &\leq x_n^0,\ n = 1, \ldots, N, \\
z_k &\geq 0,\ k = 1, \ldots, K,
\end{aligned}
$$

which is the numerator for $Q_u(x^0, y^0, u^k, u^l)$. The denominator is computed by replacing $u^{k'}$ on the right hand side of the bad output constraint with the observed bad outputs for the year 1971, i.e., u^0. As above, this problem constructs the best practice frontier from the observed data and computes the scaling factor on bad outputs required for each country to attain best practice.[14]

Leaving aside the disaggregated outcomes obtained using the methodology described above, in Table 1 below we provide the average values. In Table 1, for each index, the first columns show the geometric mean of the index between 1971 and 1990 and measure the average performance of an individual country with respect to the base year 1971. The second columns are reserved for the average annual growth rate of each index. Our comparative analysis will be based on the average performance indicators evaluated with respect to the base year. Starting from the bottom of the table, the mean environmental performance index (overall index), averaged over all the countries in the sample, indicates that over the years 1971-1990 OECD countries could have successfully expanded their desirable output to undesirable output ratio by 11%. The good output quantity index averages 34.9% and the bad output quantity index averages 21.5%. Individual country performances indicate that, while Iceland, Sweden and France were the leaders in expanding their good output over the bad outputs, Mexico, Turkey and Greece were the worst

[14]Note that this index measures the environmental performance of each country relative to itself in 1971. Its advantage is that it does not require any assumptions about cross country technology. However, if the interest is in the cross-country comparisons of environmental efficiency levels, one can assume the same technology for all the countries and let $k = 1, \ldots, K$ index the countries in the sample. Then, a reasonable benchmark would be a hypothetical country constructed as the mean of the data, and the resultant efficiency scores will provide a cross country comparison relative to the mean. See Färe, Grosskopf and Hernandez-Sancho (2004) for an alternative approach in their application.

performers in this respect.

It is well known that during the past two decades the developed countries have made important efforts in reducing emissions of pollutants. However, as the results in Table 1 suggest, these have not been equally important for all OECD countries. In this regard, the classification of countries into those that performed better than average and those below the average with respect to the overall environmental performance indicator sheds light on the relative importance attached to environmental concerns while pursuing growth objectives.

A comparison of the average indicators reveals that relatively low income countries, as measured by average per-capita GDP between 1971-1990 expressed in international prices (1985 U.S. dollars), while trying to catch-up with relatively high income countries may have ignored environmental concerns. Note that while these countries achieved higher growth rates for the good output than high income countries, their emissions of pollutants have increased at an even faster rate, lowering their environmental performance below 1971 levels. The relatively high income countries are the ones which achieved lower than average growth in good output with rather low (and in 5 cases with negative) growth rates in bad output (again evaluated with respect to the base year 1971). This is an indication that environmental concerns are becoming a binding constraint only after a certain level of income is reached and this can be best addressed in an Environmental Kuznets Curve context using panel data, to which we turn next.

Letting E_{it} represent the environmental performance of country i in year t, the equation below specifies a possible relation between environmental performance and per-capita GDP (GDPPC):

$$E_{it} = \beta_{1i} + \beta_2 GDPPC_{it} + \beta_3 (GDPPC)^2_{it} + \beta_4 (GDPPC)^3_{it} + \epsilon_{it}$$

where: i: country index; t: time index; ϵ: disturbance term with mean zero and finite variance. The shape of the polynomial will reveal the relationship between environmental efficiency and GDP per capita. A negative sign for GDPPC coupled with a positive sign for its quadratic and a negative sign for its cubic terms will imply deteriorating environmental performance at the initial phases of growth which is followed by a phase of improvement and then a further deterioration once a critical level of per capita GDP is reached.

Table I. Average environmental performance Indicators

	Good Index		*Bad Index*		*Overall Index*		*GDP/pop*
	Avg.	Annl Growth	Avg.	Annl Growth	Avg.	Annl Growth	71-90 Avg. (85 $)
High perf.							
Iceland	1.565	3.9	1.087	-0.6	1.440	4.6	10968
Sweden	1.199	1.9	0.881	-1.0	1.361	2.9	12644
France	1.281	2.4	0.977	-0.3	1.310	2.7	11650
Belgium	1.273	2.3	0.976	-1.0	1.304	3.3	10799
Canada	1.475	3.5	1.133	0.9	1.301	2.5	14181
Japan	1.497	4.1	1.154	1.7	1.297	2.3	10404
UK	1.229	2.3	0.997	0.1	1.233	2.2	10622
Neth.	1.252	2.2	1.041	0.5	1.203	1.8	11112
Italy	1.349	2.8	1.137	1.5	1.187	1.4	9963
USA	1.287	2.5	1.097	0.5	1.174	2.0	15550
Denmark	1.217	1.9	1.038	0.9	1.173	1.0	11769
Ireland	1.472	3.8	1.256	2.1	1.172	1.7	6790
Finland	1.369	3.1	1.218	1.3	1.124	1.8	10950
Switz.	1.090	1.4	0.978	0.2	1.114	1.2	14318
Average	1.319		1.064		1.239		11551
Low perf.							
Norway	1.484	3.4	1.415	2.5	1.049	0.9	11999
Austria	1.317	2.6	1.299	3.0	1.014	-0.4	10281
Germany	1.223	2.2	1.230	3.4	0.994	-1.2	11740
Australia	1.329	2.8	1.355	3.1	0.981	-0.2	12646
New Zeal.	1.230	1.7	1.270	1.8	0.968	-0.1	10858
Spain	1.356	3.0	1.424	2.8	0.952	0.2	7575
Portugal	1.479	4.2	1.559	4.2	0.949	0.0	5052
Mexico	1.608	4.0	1.713	4.0	0.939	0.0	5297
Turkey	1.566	4.6	1.808	5.8	0.866	-1.1	2992
Greece	1.381	2.8	1.673	4.9	0.825	-2.0	5790
Average	1.392		1.462		0.952		8423
Grand Mn.	1.349		1.215		1.110		10248

Notes: Annual growth is average annual percent.

Models that combine cross-section and time-series data rely on the premise that differences across units can be captured in differences in the intercept term. However estimation techniques differ with respect to the nature of assumptions made on the intercept of the equation. If the β_{1i} are assumed to be fixed parameters, then the model is known as a fixed effects model. If on the other hand the β_{1i} are assumed to be random variables that are expressed as $\beta_{1i} = \widehat{\beta}_1 + \mu_i$, where $\widehat{\beta}_1$ is an unknown parameter and μ_i are independent and identically distributed random variables with mean zero and constant variance, then the model is called a random effects model. The disadvantage of the fixed effects model is that there are too many parameters to be estimated and hence loss of degrees of freedom which can be avoided if we either assume the same intercept for all the cross sectional units, or assume β_{1i} to be random variables. Nevertheless, the random effects model is not totally free from problems. In cases where μ_i and other independent variables are correlated, the random effects model is similar to an omitted variable specification which will lead to biased parameter estimates, making a fixed effects model a more appropriate choice. In examining the relationship between our environmental performance index and per-capita GDP, we will perform the relevant tests to determine the most suitable estimation form.

Table 2 below provides the parameter estimates of the regressions for the E index under alternative specifications where column one and two provide the parameter estimates of the fixed effects model with a common intercept and fixed effects model with country specific intercepts respectively. The third column is reserved for the parameter estimates of the random effects model. An F test performed on the alternative specifications of the fixed effects model rejects the null hypothesis of a common intercept in favor of the model with country specific intercept terms. Furthermore, the choice between the fixed effects model and the random effects model can be made using the Hausman test. The Hausman test has an asymptotic $\chi^2_{(k-1)}$ distribution and in this particular case we fail to reject the null hypothesis which suggests that the random effects model is the appropriate specification.[15] So our preferred model is the random effects model.

The most apparent outcome in all the specifications of the model is that GDP per capita, its quadratic and cubic terms are always statistically significant and their respective signs imply deteriorating environmental performance at the initial phases of growth (up to an income

[15]Hausman test statistics test for the orthogonality of the random effects and the regressors, i.e., $H_0 : E(\mu_i|x_{it}) = 0$. Failure to reject this null, is failure to reject no correlation between μ_i and regressors. In this case the preferred specification is the random effects model since the random effects estimator is a best linear unbiased estimator once H_0 is satisfied. Our test statistic $\chi^2_{(3)} = 2.665$ is less than the critical value 7.82 at 5% significance level and fails to reject the null hypothesis.

level of approximately $6000 according to both the fixed effect model and the random effects model) which is followed by a phase of improvement and then a further deterioration once a critical level of per capita GDP (approximately $21000) is reached. This is actually another representation of the environmental Kuznets curve relationship where the initial deterioration of environmental conditions and its improvement in latter stages of economic growth manifest itself as an initial decline and then an improvement of environmental efficiency as measured by our index. The upper turning point is slightly beyond the sample range indicating that there may be negative repercussions on environmental performance after this level of income is reached[16]

How do these results compare to those obtained in other studies? Direct comparisons are difficult since our index is a composite one which includes both carbon dioxide and solid particulate matter, while other studies reported results for each pollutant individually. Studies almost unanimously agree that carbon dioxide emissions are monotonically increasing with income. For solid particulate matter, results reported vary from steadily declining emissions in Grossman and Krueger (1995) to improving environmental conditions after $11217 per capita GDP in Selden and Song (1994) and $4500 in Panayotou (1993). Our results, which simultaneously account for carbon dioxide and solid particulate matter, suggest that environmental performance deteriorates until per capita income reaches approximately $6000, i.e., our turning point falls between the Selden and Song (1994) and Panayotou (1993) estimates.

6.3 Concluding Remarks

In this section we employed an index number approach to measure environmental performance in OECD countries between 1971 and 1990. This approach, which relies on the construction of a quantity index of good outputs and a quantity index of bad outputs by putting due emphasis on the distinctive characteristics of production with negative externalities, provides a means of simultaneously accounting for multiple

[16]When a Kuznets curve is sought over an alternative environmental performance index for which the computation strategy is described in footnote 7, this provides additional insight on the robustness of the results. A pooled regression of type $E_{ti} = \beta_{t1} + \beta_2 GDPPC_{ti} + \beta_3 (GDPPC)^2_{ti} + \beta_4 (GDPPC)^3_{ti} + \epsilon_{ti}$ where the constant term now captures any year specific effects on this alternative environmental performance index, yields the same 'sign ordering' as in regressions in Table 1 for the (quite significant) parameter estimates. The relevant hypothesis test, by rejecting any year specific effects, favors a common intercept model. The turning points with this new specification are $7439 and $15925.

Table 2 Parameter estimates for alternative models
Environmental Performance Index

	Constant Intercept	*Fixed Effects*[a]	*Random Effects*
Constant	0.9726	1.5088	1.436
	(14.201)		(6.896)
GDPPC	-3.96E-05	-0.000232	-0.000203
	(-1.514)	(-7.231)	(-3.349)
$(GDPPC)^2$	7.29E-09	2.45E-08	2.18E-08
	(2.445)	(7.687)	(3.810)
$(GDPPC)^3$	-2.05E-13	-6.01E-13	-5.30E-13
	(-1.950)	(-5.959)	(-3.074)
R^{2b}	0.275	0.687	0.684
R^{2c}	0.938	0.968	0.661
Homogeneity test		25.39	
(DF)		(23, 453)	
Hausman test stat.			2.665
(DF)			(3)
Turning Points	$3129	$6107	$5998
	$20578	$21069	$20925
N	480	480	480

[a] Constant terms include the mean of the estimated country effects.
[b] R^2 of the unweighted regression.
[c] R^2 of the weighted regression.

pollutants within a production theoretic framework.

Our results suggest that efforts in reducing emissions of pollutants have not been equally important for all OECD countries; relatively low income countries are generally lagging behind high income countries in this regard. While lower income countries achieved higher growth rates on average for the good output than high income countries, their emissions of pollutants have increased at an even faster rate, lowering their environmental performance below 1971 levels.

A formal analysis that establishes the link between economic growth and environmental performance reveals that there exists a critical level of per capita income of approximately $6000 above which environmental performance increases. This result provides further evidence for the existence of an environmental Kuznets type relationship between per capita GDP and our environmental index which simultaneously accounts for multiple pollutants.

7. Remarks on the Literature

The notions of weak disposability and null-jointness may be traced back to Shephard and Färe (1974). See also Färe and Grosskopf (1983a,b) for early efforts at measuring congestion and modeling output sets with byproducts; these early efforts typically employed Shephard type distance functions. Färe, Grosskopf, Lovell and Pasurka (1989) struggled with alternate nonparametric specifications of performance measures in the presence of undesirable outputs, including a hyperbolic measure that is very close to the directional distance function which was not employed in this literature until later. Similarly, Färe, Grosskopf, Lovell and Yaisawarng (1993) used Shephard type distance functions as a basis for shadow pricing undesirable outputs.

The directional distance function approach to modeling and measuring performance in the presence of undesirable outputs may be traced back to a series of theoretical and empirical papers and a dissertation by Y.H. Chung. See Chambers, Chung and Färe (1998) and Chung, Färe, and Grosskopf (1997). The shadow price model based on directional distance functions is discussed in Färe and Grosskopf (1998) and has been applied in Ball, Färe, Grosskopf and Nehring (2001) and Färe, Grosskopf and Weber (2001a,b).

Although not discussed in detail in this essay, some work has been done on modeling the effects of regulation on profitability, particularly in the nonparametric, DEA framework, see Brännlund, Färe and Grosskopf (1995). Brännlund, Chung, Färe and Grosskopf (1998) extend this model to simulate introduction of emissions trading in the Swedish paper and pulp industry.

The network model approach includes the early paper included here by Färe, Grosskopf and Lee. See Färe and Grosskopf (1996) for a general discussion of network models.

8. Appendix: Proofs

Proof of (2.21)
Assume that

(i) $\frac{D_y(x^o,y^k,u^o)}{D_y(x^o,y^l,u^o)} = \frac{D_y(x^1,y^k,u^1)}{D_y(x^1,y^l,u^1)}$.
then

$$D_y(x^o, y^k, u^o) = D_y(x^o, y^l, u^o)\frac{D_y(x^1, y^k, u^1)}{D_y(x^1, y^l, u^1)}.$$

Define

$$H(x^o, u^o) = D_y(x^o, y^l, u^o)$$

and

$$F(y^k) = \frac{D_y(x^1, y^k, u^1)}{D_y(x^1, y^l, u^1)},$$

by fixing (y^l, x^1, u^1), then we may write

(ii) $D_y(x^o, y^k, u^o) = H(x^o, u^o)F(y^k)$.
Now set $y^k = 1$, then

(iii) $H(x^o, u^o) = \frac{D_y(x^o,1,u^o)}{F(1)}$.
Insert (iii) into (ii), then

(iv) $D_y(x^o, y^k, u^o) = D_y(x^o, 1, u^o)\frac{F(y^k)}{F(1)}$.
Now set $x^o = u^o = 1$, then

(v) $D_y(1, y^k, 1) = D_y(1, 1, 1)\frac{F(y^k)}{F(1)}$.
From (iv) and (v) we get

(vi) $D_y(x^o, y^k, u^o) = \frac{D_y(x^o,1,u^o)}{D_y(1,1,1)}D_y(1, y^k, 1)$.

Conversely, if (vi) holds so does (i), completing the proof.
Q.E.D.

Chapter 3

ESSAY 3: AGGREGATION ISSUES

In this essay we study various issues related to aggregation of efficiency and productivity measures. The reader is referred to Blackorby, Primont and Russell (1978) for a general theoretical treatment of aggregation and separability in the context of modern microeconomic theory. The general idea is to find conditions on the fundamentals of technology or preferences which allow us to infer aggregate outcomes or performance measures (in our case) from individual measures of performance, for example.

Of course, the individual performance measures we have been discussing are themselves a type of aggregator function, summarizing or aggregating many attributes into a single number, often in the absence of prices, which for economists are the most natural tools to use in aggregating 'apples and oranges.' Instead of aggregating the many aspects of production of a single decision-making unit or producer into a single performance measure, here we begin by focusing on aggregating the individual performance measures up to a group or industry performance measure. For example, we ask: When can we simply 'add up' the individual measures—or take an average—to get a consistent measure of overall industry performance? As it turns out, aggregation of firm performance which is consistent with industry performance will require that we pay attention to the 'functional form' of the performance measures we are using. This general idea is illustrated with our opening motivating section on the Fox paradox.

The next sections go back to the indicators and indexes from Essay 1, and specifically derive conditions for consistent aggregation for each case. The overall performance measures–for example the Nerlovian Profit indicator–are typically price dependent and lend themselves to adaptations of the aggregation result due to Koopmans (1957) concerning profit functions. The component measures, especially the technical efficiency components are less straightforward. We also include a discussion of aggregation using the Johansen approach and for Luenberger productivity indicators.

The next theoretical section addresses a different type of aggregation; namely, consistency of efficiency measures when we wish to aggregate across inputs or outputs. This is followed by a section devoted to maintaining consistency of the various decompositions when we wish to aggregate or average. We end the essay with an empirical application of profit efficiency and aggregation by Fukuyama and Weber.

1. The Fox Paradox

The purpose of this section is to show that the way efficiency indicators or indexes are defined and the way that the efficiency scores are aggregated are interdependent. A useful illustration arises from the Fox Paradox raised by K. Fox (1999). The essence of the paradox is that even if one firm produces each of two outputs more efficiently than another firm, when outputs are aggregated the first firm may be overall less efficient than the second.

To illustrate the paradox and how one may 'outfox' it, suppose that there are two firms $k = 1,2$ each producing two outputs $m = 1,2$. Let c_{km} be the observed or actual cost of producing output m by firm k, and let $\hat{c}_{km}$ be the predicted or minimum cost. The efficiency of firm k in producing output m equals the ratio

$$\hat{c}_{km}/c_{km}, k = 1,2\ m = 1,2. \tag{3.1}$$

Total cost for each firm is the sum of individual output costs, i.e.,

$$c_{k1} + c_{k2} \text{ and } \hat{c}_{k1} + \hat{c}_{k2}, k = 1,2, \tag{3.2}$$

are the total observed and minimum cost, respectively for each firm.

Overall efficiency for each firm is defined as

$$(\hat{c}_{k1} + \hat{c}_{k2})/(c_{k1} + c_{k2}),\ k = 1,2. \tag{3.3}$$

The Fox Paradox states that is possible that

$$(\hat{c}_{11}/c_{11}) > (\hat{c}_{21}/c_{21}) \text{ and } (\hat{c}_{12}/c_{12}) > (\hat{c}_{22}/c_{22})$$

but

$$(\hat{c}_{11} + \hat{c}_{12})/(c_{11} + c_{12}) < (\hat{c}_{21} + \hat{c}_{22})/(c_{21} + c_{22}),$$

i.e., firm 1 is more efficient than firm 2 in producing each output separately, but it is overall less efficient than firm 2.

Why does this paradox arise? As it turns out, the way in which efficiency is measured at the disaggregated level and the way in which the scores are aggregated are incompatible, causing the paradox. Since we feel that it is very natural to aggregate cost and other value measures by adding them together, we would like to maintain the additive aggregation and find a measure of efficiency that will yield consistent additive aggregation. To keep things fairly general, we seek an efficiency measure that is a continuous function of minimum and observed cost, i.e.,

$$\Gamma(\hat{c}_{km}, c_{km}),\ k = 1, 2,\ m = 1, 2. \tag{3.4}$$

Then we assume that the efficiency scores for each firm can be summed consistently, i.e., which is how we avoid the paradox. This is achieved by requiring that

$$\Gamma(\hat{c}_{k1}, c_{k1}) + \Gamma(\hat{c}_{k2}, c_{k2}) = \Gamma(\hat{c}_{k1} + \hat{c}_{k2}, c_{k1} + c_{k2}),\ k = 1, 2. \tag{3.5}$$

Now if

$$\Gamma(\hat{c}_{1m}, c_{1m}) > \Gamma(\hat{c}_{2m}, c_{2m}),\ m = 1, 2, \tag{3.6}$$

then

$$\Gamma(\hat{c}_{11} + \hat{c}_{12}, c_{11} + c_{12}) > \Gamma(\hat{c}_{21} + \hat{c}_{22}, c_{21} + c_{22}). \tag{3.7}$$

In words, if firm 1 is more efficient than firm 2 in producing each output it is also overall more efficient. This is the consistency criteria we impose to avoid the paradox.

It remains to find a form for the efficiency measure that satisfies these criteria, i.e., we need to solve equation (3.5) above. Luckily, the solution is found in Aczél (1966, p. 215), and is written as

$$\Gamma(\hat{c}_{km}, c_{km}) = \hat{a}\hat{c}_{km} + ac_{km}. \tag{3.8}$$

Dropping the subscripts, we have

$$\Gamma(\hat{c}, c) = \hat{a}\hat{c} + ac, \tag{3.9}$$

where $\hat{a}$ and a are arbitrary constants. If we choose $\hat{a} = -1/(wg_x)$ and $a = 1/(wg_x)$, then our solution becomes

$$\Gamma(\hat{c}, c) = \frac{c - \hat{c}}{wg_x}, \tag{3.10}$$

where w is the input price vector and g_x is the directional input vector discussed in Essay 1. This expression can be interpreted as a cost efficiency indicator. The denominator serves to normalize the indicator so that it is independent of unit of measurement.

We conclude that if we wish to aggregate efficiency scores additively, then we should choose an indicator approach to measuring efficiency, i.e., the efficiency measures should have an additive rather than ratio form.

In the following sections we turn our attention to aggregation of the specific indicators and indexes that were introduced in Essay 1. But first we study some important results based on work by Koopmans, which we use to derive our aggregation results.

2. A Theorem by T. C. Koopmans and Corollaries

T.C. Koopmans (1957) proved that industry maximum profit is the sum of its firms' maximum profits, i.e., aggregate profit can be derived simply by addition of individual firm profits. We use this important result to help us aggregate the Nerlovian profit indicator. In this section we also prove aggregation corollaries for the revenue and cost functions which parallel the Koopmans theorem. These will be used to derive aggregation results for the cost and revenue indicators and indexes introduced in Essay 1.

We begin by denoting firm $k's$ technology by

$$T^k = \{(x^k, y^k) : \text{ input } x^k \in \Re^N_+ \text{ can produce output } y^k \in \Re^M_+\}. \tag{3.11}$$

Here we use x^k and y^k as vectors of variables rather than as observations of data. Then the industry technology may be defined as the sum of the $k = 1, \ldots, K$ firm technologies,

$$T = \sum_{k=1}^{K} T^k = \{(x,y) : x = \sum_{k=1}^{K} x^k, y = \sum_{k=1}^{K} y^k, (x^k, y^k) \in T^k, k = 1, \ldots, K\}. \tag{3.12}$$

Now we define the firm profit function as

$$\Pi^k(p,w) = \max\{py^k - wx^k : (x^k, y^k) \in T^k\} \tag{3.13}$$

and the industry profit function as

$$\Pi(p,w) = \max\{py - wx : (x,y) \in T\}, \tag{3.14}$$

where $p \in \Re_+^M$ is a vector of output prices and $w \in \Re_+^N$ is a vector of input prices.

Koopmans' theorem states that the sum of the firm maximal profits equals the industry maximum profit, i.e.,

Theorem (Koopmans): $\Pi(p,w) = \sum_{k=1}^{K} \Pi^k(p,w), (p,w) \geqq 0.$

The proof is to be found in the appendix.

We illustrate the theorem for the simple two firm case, where each produces one unit of output, one using one unit of input (T^a) and one using two units of input (T^b). See Figure 3.1.

The profit maximizing input-output vector for the first firm is at a where the firm uses 1 unit of input to produce 1 unit of output, and for the second firm it is at b using 2 units of input to produce 1 unit of output. The sum of these optimizers is at c (with $x = 3$ and $y = 2$) which is the profit maximizing bundle for the industry, i.e.,

$$(p1 - w1) + (p1 - w2) = p2 - w3. \tag{3.15}$$

Next we turn to the firm and industry revenue functions and demonstrate that a similar relationship holds. Instead of characterizing technology with T^k we turn to the output sets, for each firm k (again, where x^k, y^k are variables)

$$P^k(x^k) = \{y^k : x^k \text{ can produce } y^k\} = \{y^k : (x^k, y^k) \in T^k\}. \tag{3.16}$$

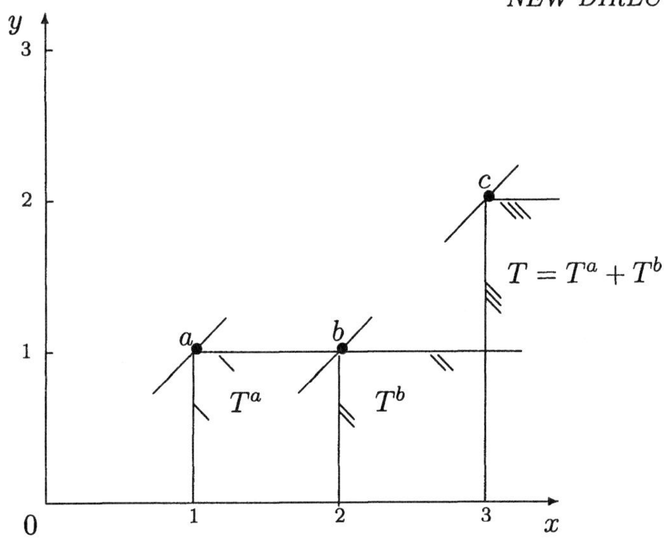

Figure 3.1. Koopmans' Theorem

The associated industry output set is defined as the sum of the firm output sets, namely

$$P(x^1, \ldots, x^K) = \sum_{k=1}^{K} P^k(x^k). \tag{3.17}$$

The industry output set $P(x^1, \ldots, x^K)$ incorporates the individual firm technologies $P^k(x^k)$ and the allocation of inputs across the firms $(x^1, \ldots, x^K)$. This industry model differs from the profit industry model in that here inputs are not aggregated across firms (see the definition of industry technology T above). The industry output set depends on the allocation of inputs since these are given for each firm.

Recall that the revenue function for each firm seeks maximum revenue by choosing outputs y given inputs x and output prices p such that

$$R^k(x^k, p) = \max\{py^k : y^k \in P^k(x^k)\}. \tag{3.18}$$

We may now state the revenue version of Koopmans' theorem (the proof is in the appendix).

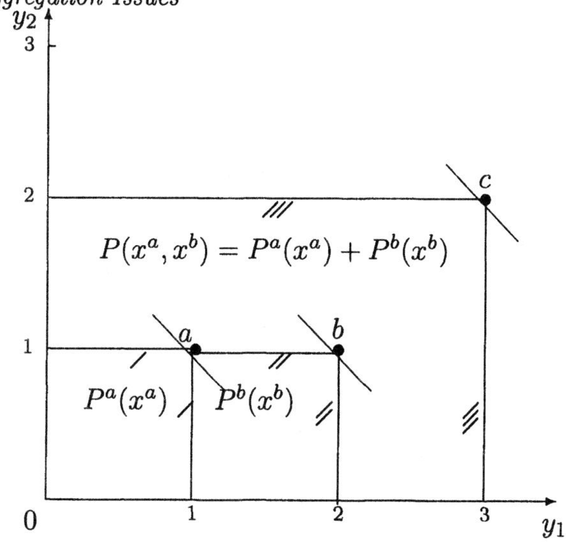

Figure 3.2. The Revenue Aggregation Theorem

Revenue Corollary: $R(x^1, \ldots, x^K, p) = \sum_{k=1}^{K} R^k(x^k, p), p \in \Re_+^M$, where the industry revenue function is given by $R(x^1, \ldots, x^K, p) = \max\{py : y \in P(x^1, \ldots, x^K)\}$.

This Corollary demonstrates that industry revenue is the sum of the firm revenues, which we illustrate below.

In our figure we have two firms with associated output sets $P^k(x^k), k = 1, 2$, each of which produces two outputs. Firm 1 maximizes its revenue at a with $y_1 = 1$ and $y_2 = 1$ and firm 2 maximizes its revenue at b with $y_1 = 2$ and $y_2 = 1$. The industry revenue maximization takes place where $y_1 = 3$ and $y_2 = 2$ at c and that revenue is equal to the sum of the firm revenues, i.e.,

$$(p_1 1 + p_2 1) + (p_1 2 + p_2 1) = p_1 3 + p_2 2. \tag{3.19}$$

To formulate the cost version of Koopmans' theorem, define the industry input requirement set as the sum of the associated firm input sets.

$$L(y^1, \ldots, y^K) = \sum_{k=1}^{K} L^k(y^k), \tag{3.20}$$

where

$$L^k(y^k) = \{x^k : x^k \text{ can produce } y^k\} = \{x^k : (x^k, y^k) \in T^k\}. \tag{3.21}$$

In contrast to the aggregation of the technologies T^k for the profit case, here outputs are not aggregated, thus the industry set $L(y^1, \ldots, y^K)$ depends on the distribution of individual firm output vectors. This is consistent with the definition of the cost function which seeks to minimize cost by choosing inputs *given* the allocation of outputs and input prices, i.e., the cost function for firm k is

$$C^k(y^k, w) = \min\{wx^k : x^k \in L^k(y^k)\} \tag{3.22}$$

and the industry cost function is

$$C(y^1, \ldots, y^K, w) = \min\{wx : x \in L(y^1, \ldots, y^K)\}. \tag{3.23}$$

The cost version of Koopmans' theorem reads

Cost Corollary : $C(y^1, \ldots, y^K, w) = \sum_{k=1}^{K} C^k(y^k, w), w \in \Re_+^N.$

This corollary echoes the message of the original theorem: taking the sum of the individual firm's optimization—here cost minimization—yields the industry optimization.

3. Aggregating Indicators Across Firms

In this section we show how the three efficiency indicators (and their component measures) discussed in Essay 1 can be aggregated across firms to form an industry indicator. The fundamental tools we use in this process are Koopmans' theorem and its corollaries, which have in common with the indicators their additive structure.

Suppose we have $k = 1, \ldots, K$ firm observations of inputs and outputs (x^k, y^k). Then observed industry inputs and outputs are their sums,

$$x = \sum_{k=1}^{K} x^k \text{ and } y = \sum_{k=1}^{K} y^k. \tag{3.24}$$

Recall from Essay 1 that the **Nerlovian Profit Indicator** for firm k may be written as

$$\frac{\Pi^k(p,w) - (py^k - wx^k)}{pg_y + wg_x},$$

where $\Pi^k(p,w)$ is maximal profit for firm k and $(py^k - wx^k)$ is its observed or actual profit. The difference between these values is normalized by the value of the directional vector (g_y, g_x). This normalization renders the indicator independent of unit of the currency in which the prices are given.

Consistent with the firm indicator we may define an industry level counterpart, the **Nerlovian Industry Profit Indicator** as

$$\frac{\Pi(p,w) - (p\sum_{k=1}^{K} y^k - w\sum_{k=1}^{K} x^k)}{pg_y + wg_x}, \tag{3.25}$$

where

$$\Pi(p,w) = \max\{py - wx : (x,y) \in T = \sum_{k=1}^{K} T^k\} \tag{3.26}$$

is the .

From Koopmans' theorem we know that the industry maximal profit is the sum of its firms' maximal profits:

$$\Pi(p,w) = \sum_{k=1}^{K} \Pi^k(p,w). \tag{3.27}$$

Using this theorem in connection with the profit indicator for the industry we have

$$\frac{\Pi(p,w) - (p\sum_{k=1}^{K} y^k - w\sum_{k=1}^{K} x^k)}{pg_y + wg_x} = \sum_{k=1}^{K} \frac{\Pi^k(p,w) - (py^k - wx^k)}{pg_y + wg_x}. \tag{3.28}$$

Thus the sum of the firm profit indicators yields the industry indicator. Note that the difference between maximal and observed profit is normalized by $(pg_y + wg_x)$, and this normalization is the same for the firms and the industry.

Blackorby and Russell (1999) introduced the **Axiom of Aggregate Indication** which in the case of Nerlovian Profit Efficiency may be written

$$\frac{\Pi(p,w) - (p\sum_{k=1}^{K} y^k - w\sum_{k=1}^{K} x^k)}{pg_y + wg_x} = 0$$

if and only if

$$\frac{\Pi^k(p,w) - (py^k - wx^k)}{pg_y + wg_x} = 0, k = 1, \ldots, K.$$

In words, the industry is efficient if and only if each firm is efficient. Since each indicator is nonnegative we can conclude that the Nerlovian industry profit indicator has this property.

In order to address aggregation of the technical efficiency component of profit efficiency, define the industry directional technology distance function as

$$\vec{D}_T(\sum_{k=1}^{K} x^k, \sum_{k=1}^{K} y^k; g_x, g_y) = \sup\{\beta : (\sum_{k=1}^{K} x^k - \beta g_x, \sum_{k=1}^{K} y^k + \beta g_y) \in T\}. \tag{3.29}$$

Then from Essay 1 the industry profit indicator can be decomposed into allocative and technical components, i.e,

$$\frac{\Pi(p,w) - (p\sum_{k=1}^{K} y^k - w\sum_{k=1}^{K} x^k)}{pg_y + wg_x} = \vec{D}_T(\sum_{k=1}^{K} x^k, \sum_{k=1}^{K} y^k; g_x, g_y) + \vec{AE}_T. \tag{3.30}$$

The distance function $\vec{D}_T(\sum_{k=1}^{K} x^k, \sum_{k=1}^{K} y^k; g_x, g_y)$ measures technical efficiency and the residual $\vec{AE}_T$ captures the allocative component.

The corresponding decomposition for a firm k is

$$\frac{\Pi^k(p,w) - (py^k - wx^k)}{pg_y + wg_x} = \vec{D}_{T^k}(x^k, y^k; g_x, g_y) + \vec{AE}_{T^k}, k = 1, \ldots, K. \tag{3.31}$$

Now expressions (3.28), (3.30) and (3.31) yield

$$\vec{D}_T(\textstyle\sum_{k=1}^K x^k, \sum_{k=1}^K y^k; g_x, g_y) = \sum_{k=1}^K \vec{D}_{T^k}(x^k, y^k; g_x, g_y)$$

if and only if

$$\vec{AE}_T = \textstyle\sum_{k=1}^K \vec{AE}_{T^k}.$$

That is, the technical efficiency component aggregates if and only if the allocative component aggregates. This is verified by the equality

$$\vec{D}_T(\sum_{k=1}^K x^k, \sum_{k=1}^K y^k; g_x, g_y) + \vec{AE}_T = \sum_{k=1}^K \vec{D}_{T^k}(x^k, y^k; g_x, g_y) + \sum_{k=1}^K \vec{AE}_{T^k}. \tag{3.32}$$

Suppose we do not impose or know whether the allocative efficiency component aggregates. Then we still have the following inequality

$$\vec{D}_T(\sum_{k=1}^K x^k, \sum_{k=1}^K y^k; g_x, g_y) \geqq \sum_{k=1}^K \vec{D}_{T^k}(x^k, y^k; g_x, g_y). \tag{3.33}$$

This says that the sum of the firm technical efficiency components is a lower bound on industry technical efficiency.

This result follows from the definition of the industry technology

$$T = \textstyle\sum_{k=1}^K T^k$$

and the observation that

$$\textstyle\sum_{k=1}^K (x^k - \vec{D}_{T^k}(x^k, y^k; g_x, g_y)g_x, y^k + \vec{D}_{T^k}(x^k, y^k; g_x, g_y)g_y) =$$
$$(\textstyle\sum_{k=1}^K x^k - \sum_{k=1}^K \vec{D}_{T^k}(x^k, y^k; g_x, g_y)g_x,$$

$\sum_{k=1}^{K} y^k + \sum_{k=1}^{K} \vec{D}_{T^k}(x^k, y^k; g_x, g_y)g_y) \in T$.

Note further that (3.32) and (3.33) yield the inequality

$\sum_{k=1}^{K} \vec{AE}_{T^k} \geqq \vec{AE}_T,$

and in particular if each firm is allocatively efficient, i.e., $\vec{AE}_{T^k} = 0, k = 1, \ldots, K$, then since $\vec{AE}_T \geqq 0$, the industry is allocatively efficient as well. (We thank Jesus Pastor who first provided us with a proof).

To summarize: we have shown that the profit indicator aggregates and its technical component also aggregates provided that the allocative component aggregates. Moreover, this would also be the case if each firm is allocatively efficient. Finally we note that even in the absence of any assumption about allocative efficiency, the industry technical efficiency component is bounded from below by the sum of the firm components.

So far we have been thinking about aggregation in the context of an optimization problem and focusing on the optimizers. What happens if we insist on aggregation of any possible input and output vector? If we assume that the technical efficiency component aggregates for all $x^k \in \Re_+^N$ and $y^k \in \Re_+^M$ and let (g_x, g_y) be the unit vector, then the condition that the firm technical efficiency components aggregate to the industry technical efficiency component is a Pexider functional equation in many variables. The solution to this equation is (see Aczél, 1966, p. 302)

$$\vec{D}_{T^k}(x^k, y^k; 1, 1) = \sum_{n=1}^{N} a_n x_{kn} + \sum_{m=1}^{M} b_m y_{km} + c_k, k = 1, \ldots, K, \quad (3.34)$$

and

$$\vec{D}_T(\sum_{k=1}^{K} x^k, \sum_{k=1}^{K} y^k; 1, 1) = \sum_{n=1}^{N} a_n \sum_{k=1}^{K} x_{kn} + \sum_{m=1}^{M} b_m \sum_{k=1}^{K} y_{km} + \sum_{k=1}^{K} c_k, \quad (3.35)$$

where a_n, b_m and c_k are arbitrary constants. Thus this solution shows that the technology must be linear if consistent aggregation of technical efficiency should hold for all $x^k \in \Re_+^N$ and $y^k \in \Re_+^M$, and the only difference across firms is the intercept coefficient c_k. This is essentially the pessimistic conclusion reached by Blackorby and Russell,(1999) which we would expect since instead of focusing on optimizing bundles of inputs and outputs, we are seeking the solution for any possible input and output combination.

Furthermore if we take account of the fact that the directional technology distance functions $\vec{D}_T^k$ and $\vec{D}_T$ must satisfy the translation property, our result is even more restrictive. Recall from Essay 1 that this property states

$$\vec{D}_T(x - \alpha g_x, y + \alpha g_y; g_x, g_y) = \vec{D}_T(x, y; g_x, g_y) - \alpha,$$

i.e., the translation of inputs and outputs reduces the value of the distance function by the size of the translation.

In our case $\vec{D}_{T^k}$ and $\vec{D}_T$ satisfy this property provided

$$\sum_{m=1}^{M} b_m - \sum_{n=1}^{N} a_n = -1.$$

Turning next to aggregation of the revenue and cost indicators, it is natural to use the results that the industry revenue and cost functions are the sum of the associated firm functions. In parallel with our result for profit functions, we know that the industry revenue function is the sum of its firm's revenue functions

$$R(x^1, \ldots, x^K, p) = \sum_{k=1}^{K} R^k(x^k, p). \tag{3.36}$$

If we define industry output as

$$y = \sum_{k=1}^{K} y^k, \tag{3.37}$$

where y^k is the output for firm k, then we can define the **Industry Revenue Indicator** as

$$\frac{R(x^1,\ldots,x^K,p)-p\sum_{k=1}^K y^k}{pg_y},$$

which we use to obtain the following equality,

$$\frac{R(x^1,\ldots,x^K,p)-p\sum_{k=1}^K y^k}{pg_y} = \sum_{k=1}^K \frac{R^k(x^k,p)-py^k}{pg_y}. \tag{3.38}$$

The left-hand-side of this expression is the industry revenue indicator which is the sum of the individual firm indicators on the right-hand-side. In other words, the individual revenue indicators aggregate additively to equal the industry revenue indicator, which is a consequence—as for the profit indicators—of the Koopmans' relationship; in this case the revenue corollary.

In Essay 1 we show that the revenue indicator consists of a technical and an allocative component; for the industry this may be written as

$$\frac{R(x^1,\ldots,x^K,p)-p\sum_{k=1}^K y^k}{pg_y} = \vec{D}_o(x^1,\ldots,x^K,\sum_{k=1}^K y^k;g_y)+\vec{AE}_o \tag{3.39}$$

and for the firms as

$$\frac{R^k(x^k,p)-py^k}{pg_y} = \vec{D}_o^k(x^k,y^k;g_y)+\vec{AE}_o^k. \tag{3.40}$$

Since from above we know that the revenue indicators aggregate consistently from firm to industry we may substitute and derive the following relationship

$$\vec{D}_o(x^1,\ldots,x^K,\sum_{k=1}^K y^k;g_y)+\vec{AE}_o = \sum_{k=1}^K \vec{D}_o^k(x^k,y^k;g_y)+\sum_{k=1}^K \vec{AE}_o^k, \tag{3.41}$$

where the left-hand side is the industry decomposition and the right-hand side is the sum of the firm's decompositions.

The next step is to determine under what conditions the technical and allocative components aggregate separately. It follows that the technical component aggregates if and only if the allocative efficiency component aggregates, i.e.,

$$\vec{D}_o(x^1,\ldots,x^K,\sum_{k=1}^{K} y^k; g_y) = \sum_{k=1}^{K} \vec{D}_o^k(x^k, y^k; g_y). \tag{3.42}$$

if and only if

$$\sum_{k=1}^{K} \vec{AE}_o^k = \vec{AE}_o.$$

In the special case of a single output there is by definition no allocative inefficiency, i.e., $\vec{AE}_o^k = \vec{AE}_o = 0, k = 1,\ldots,K$, so the technical efficiency component automatically aggregates.

To elaborate on this, recall that in the single output case the output set takes the form

$$P^k(x^k) = [0, F^k(x^k)] \tag{3.43}$$

where $F^k(x^k)$ is a production function. Now if we choose $g_y = 1$, then the directional distance function takes a simple form, namely

$$\vec{D}_o^k(x^k, y^k; 1) = F^k(x^k) - y^k.$$

This follows from

$$\begin{aligned}
\vec{D}_o^k(x^k, y^k; 1) &= \sup\{\beta : (y^k + \beta) \in [0, F^k(x^k)]\} \qquad (3.44)\\
&= \sup\{\beta : (y^k + \beta) \leq F^k(x^k)\}\\
&= F^k(x^k) - y^k.
\end{aligned}$$

The industry distance function in the case of a scalar output is

$$\vec{D}_o(x^1,\ldots,x^K,\sum_{k=1}^{K} y^k; 1) = \tag{3.45}$$

$$\sup\{\beta : (\sum_{k=1}^{K} y^k + \beta) \leqq \sum_{k=1}^{K} F^k(x^k)\}$$
$$= \sum_{k=1}^{K} F^k(x^k) - \sum_{k=1}^{K} y^k.$$

From the distance functions for the firms we see that in the single output case we have exact aggregation, i.e.,

$$\begin{aligned}\vec{D}_o(x^1, \ldots, x^K; \sum_{k=1}^{K} y^k; 1) &= \sum_{k=1}^{K} F^k(x^k) - \sum_{k=1}^{K} y^k \\ &= \sum_{k=1}^{K} (F^k(x^k) - y^k) \\ &= \sum_{k=1}^{K} \vec{D}_o^k(x^k, y^k; 1).\end{aligned}$$

Note that the industry output distance function depends on the distribution of inputs across firms; inputs are not aggregated here.

More generally, if we have more than one output or there is allocative inefficiency, then the equality above no longer holds. We do, however, find that the sum of the firm technical efficiency indicators is a lower bound on the industry technical efficiency indicator,

$$\vec{D}_o(x^1, \ldots, x^K; \sum_{k=1}^{K} y^k; 1) \geqq \sum_{k=1}^{K} \vec{D}_o^k(x^k, y^k; 1).$$

Next we turn to aggregation of the cost efficiency indicator. We have seen that by applying Koopmans' theorem and its corollaries we can aggregate the profit and revenue indicators. The same logic applies to the cost indicator as well.

We begin by defining the industry input vector as the sum of the firm input vectors, i.e,

$$x = \sum_{k=1}^{K} x^k. \tag{3.46}$$

Using the industry input vector together with the knowledge that the industry cost is the sum of firm costs, we obtain

$$\frac{w\sum_{k=1}^{K} x^k - C(y^1,\ldots,y^K,w)}{wg_x} = \sum_{k=1}^{K} \frac{wx^k - C^k(y^k,w)}{wg_x}. \tag{3.47}$$

The left-hand-side is the industry cost efficiency indicator which in turn is equal to the sum of firm cost indicators. Again the indicators aggregate exactly from firm to industry as a simple sum.

In the same way as the profit and revenue indicators, the firm technical efficiencies aggregate if and only if the industry allocative input efficiency is equal to the sum of the firm efficiencies, i.e., $\vec{AE}_i = \sum_{k=1}^{K} \vec{AE}_i^k$, so that in that case we have

$$\vec{D}_i(y^1,\ldots,y^K,\sum_{k=1}^{K} x^k; g_x) = \sum_{k=1}^{K} \vec{D}_i^k(y^k,x^k;g_x). \tag{3.48}$$

Finally, without imposing any conditions on allocative efficiency, one may prove that the industry technical input efficiency indicator is bounded below by the sum of firm technical input efficiency indicators, i.e.,

$$\vec{D}_i(y^1,\ldots,y^K,\sum_{k=1}^{K} x^k; g_x) \geqq \sum_{k=1}^{K} \vec{D}_i^k(y^k,x^k;g_x).$$

Thus we find strong symmetry in our efforts to aggregate from firm to industry; revenue, cost and profit efficiency aggregate consistently. However, the associated technical efficiency components only aggregate under conditions on allocative efficiency. Nevertheless, even without such conditions, we find that the sum of the firm technical efficiencies bound the industry technical efficiency.

4. The Johansen Approach with Extensions

So far, we have taken two different approaches to aggregation of efficiency scores across firms: i) optimize some linear functional such as profit, revenue or costs, then aggregate over the optimizers, ii) aggregate over all feasible inputs and outputs as in Blackorby and Russell (1999). The latter approach imposes restrictive conditions on the technology; in particular, technology must be linear. The first approach, on the other hand does not restrict the technology, given that we are only aggregating profit, revenue or cost indicators and not the allocative and technical efficiency components.

The Johansen approach to aggregating across firms falls somewhere between i) and ii) above in the sense that the industry output is the maximal output that can be obtained from each firm given the inputs available to the industry as a whole. The key distinguishing feature is that total industry input may be reallocated across firms to achieve this maximum output, i.e., the actual allocation of inputs to firms is ignored. This is consistent with the profit maximization model where both inputs and outputs are choice variables, but not with revenue maximization or cost minimization.

To develop the Johansen approach, we first generalize his model to accommodate our framework. Johansen formulates the single output industry production model from $k = 1, \ldots, K$ firms as

$$\begin{aligned} \max_{y_1,\ldots,y_K} \quad & \textstyle\sum_{k=1}^{K} y_k \\ s.t. \quad & \sum_{k=1}^{K} \xi_{kn} y_k \leqq x_n, n = 1, \ldots, N \\ & 0 \leqq y_k \leqq \overline{y}_k, k = 1, \ldots, K \end{aligned} \tag{3.49}$$

where $x_n = \sum_{k=1}^{K} x_{kn}$ is the industry total quantity of the $n'th$ input, found as the sum over the individual firm's usage of that input.[1] $\xi_{kn} = \overline{x}_n / \overline{y}_k$, where $\overline{x}_n$ is full capacity level of input x_n and $\overline{y}_k$ is the associated full capacity level of firm $k's$ single output.

Define $z_k = (y_k / \overline{y}_k), k = 1, \ldots, K$, then (3.50) becomes

$$\begin{aligned} \max_{z_1,\ldots,z_K} \quad & \textstyle\sum_{k=1}^{K} z_k \overline{y}_k \\ s.t. \quad & \sum_{k=1}^{K} z_k \overline{x}_{kn} \leqq x_n, n = 1, \ldots, N \\ & 0 \leqq z_k \leqq 1, k = 1, \ldots, K. \end{aligned} \tag{3.50}$$

[1] We are using the convention that subscripts are used to denote scalars or elements of a vector, and superscripts refer to a vector.

If we take $\overline{x}_{kn}$ and $\overline{y}_k$ to be observed inputs and outputs, then the formulation above is the familiar activity analysis model for a single output under an additive formulation. We may now write the generic Johansen industry model as

$$\begin{aligned} F^M(x_1,\ldots,x_N) &= \max_{x_1,\ldots,x_K} \sum_{k=1}^{K} F^k(x_{k1},\ldots,x_{kN}) \qquad (3.51) \\ & \quad s.t. \sum_{k=1}^{K} x_{kn} \leqq x_n, n = 1,\ldots,N. \end{aligned}$$

What this says is that each of our K firms has a production function $F^k(x_{k1},\ldots,x_{kN}) = F^k(x^k)$ which uses inputs x^k to produce output $F^k(x^k)$. The industry maximal output is $F^M(x_1,\ldots,x_N) = F^M(x)$, where the maximum is found over all feasible input allocations so that $\sum_{k=1}^{K} x_{kn} \leqq x_n, n = 1,\ldots,N$, where x_n is the total amount of input n available to the industry.

We illustrate the Johansen model for the simple case of one input and one output and two firms in Figure 3.3. Total input for this two firm industry is x and its allocation across firms $x^k, k = 1,2$ is specified as $x = x_1 + x_2$. Firm 1's production function is $y_1 = x_1/2$ and firm 2's is $y_2 = x_2$.

The base of the figure is the total input available to the two firms; and the firm production functions are the intersecting lines labeled $y_1 = x_1/2$ and $y_2 = x_2$. In this case it is easy to see that the allocation of input across firms that would maximize industry output is achieved for $x = x_2$ and $x_1 = 0$.

We may estimate Johansen industry output by solving the linear programming problem from above, i.e.,

$$\begin{aligned} F^M(x) = F^M(x_1,\ldots,x_N) = \max_{z_1,\ldots,z_K} & \sum_{k=1}^{K} z_k y_k \qquad (3.52) \\ s.t. & \sum_{k=1}^{K} z_k x_{kn} \leqq x_n, n = 1,\ldots,N \\ & 0 \leqq z_k \leqq 1, k = 1,\ldots,K. \end{aligned}$$

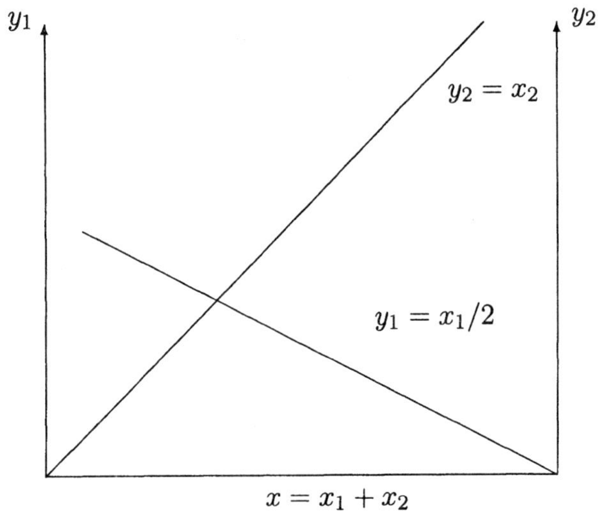

Figure 3.3. Johansen firm and industry production

If appropriate, we could introduce other constraints on the intensity variables, z_k; for example we could choose $z_k \geqq 0, k = 1, \ldots, K$ to allow for constant returns to scale. The restriction that each intensity variable lie between zero and one as in (3.52) yields an 'additive' or Koopmans technology.

Next we extend the Johansen approach in two directions: i) allowing for multiple outputs, and ii) allowing for some inputs to be firm specific. The latter extension allows for some inputs to be fixed to the firm and are therefore not available to be reallocated across the industry, which we view as a short run model.

To extend the Johansen model to the multiple output case, we first formulate the generic model in terms of directional output distance functions. It follows from (3.44) that

$$F^k(x^k) = \vec{D}_o^k(x^k, 0; 1), \text{ and } F^M(x) = \vec{D}_o^M(x, 0; 1). \tag{3.53}$$

We use this expression together with the translation property to verify this claim. It follows that

$$\vec{D}_o^M(x, 0; 1) = \max_{x^k} \sum_{k=1}^{K} \vec{D}_o^k(x^k, 0; 1) \text{ s.t. } \sum_{k=1}^{K} x^k \leqq x, \tag{3.54}$$

or by appealing to our translation property and subtracting $\sum_{k=1}^{K} y^k$ from both sides of (3.54), we have

$$\vec{D}_o^M(x, \sum_{k=1}^{K} y^k; 1) = \max_{x^k} \sum_{k=1}^{K} \vec{D}_o^k(x^k, y^k; 1) \text{ s.t. } \sum_{k=1}^{K} x^k \leqq x. \tag{3.55}$$

Now if we let $y^k \in \Re_+^M$ rather than $y^k \in \Re_+$, i.e., allow output to be a vector rather than a scalar and apply expression (3.55), we have a multiple output generalization of the Johansen approach articulated as in (3.51).

To estimate this multiple output distance function, consider the following problem

$$\begin{aligned} \vec{D}_o^M(x, \sum_{k=1}^{K} y^k; 1) &= \max\{\sum_{k=1}^{K} \beta^k : (y^k + \beta^k 1) \in P^k(x^k), \\ &\quad \text{for all } k = 1, \ldots, K, \sum_{k=1}^{K} x^k \leqq x\}. \end{aligned} \tag{3.56}$$

The solution to (3.56) yields

$$\vec{D}_o^M(x, \sum_{k=1}^{K} y^k; 1) = \sum_{k=1}^{K} \vec{D}_o^k(\hat{x}^k, y^k; 1), \tag{3.57}$$

where $\hat{x}^k$ is the optimal use of inputs in firm k and is obtained from the solution to (3.57). Since we already know how to formulate $P^k(x^k)$ as an activity analysis model it follows that this may be estimated using linear programming methods. We illustrate for the case when some inputs are firm specific, which we take up presently.

Before introducing the firm specific input case, we need to understand the relationship between $\vec{D}_o^M(x, \sum_{k=1}^{K} y^k; 1)$, where $x = \sum_{k=1}^{K} x^k$ and $\vec{D}_o(x^1, \ldots, x^K, \sum_{k=1}^{K} y^k; 1)$. The difference between the two distance functions is that $\vec{D}_o(x^1, \ldots, x^K, \sum_{k=1}^{K} y^k; 1)$ depends on the allocation of inputs across firms, while $\vec{D}_o^M(x, \sum_{k=1}^{K} y^k; 1)$ is independent of that allocation and only depends on x, i.e., the total input available to the industry.

It now follows directly that the relationship between these two distance functions may be written as

$$\vec{D}_o^M(x, \sum_{k=1}^{K} y^k; 1) \;=\; \max\{\vec{D}_o(x^1, \ldots, x^K, \sum_{k=1}^{K} y^k; 1) : \sum_{k=1}^{K} x^k \leqq x\}. \tag{3.58}$$

Thus $\vec{D}_o^M(x, \sum_{k=1}^K y^k; 1)$ is the maximum of $\vec{D}_o(x^1, \ldots, x^K, \sum_{k=1}^K y^k; 1)$ over all feasible allocations of $x^k, k = 1, \ldots, K$.

The final task in this section is to introduce firm specific inputs. One may think of these as inputs which cannot be freely allocated across firms, such as buildings, land, etc. Let $x_1, \ldots, x_{\hat{N}}, \hat{N} < N$ be such inputs and let $(N - \hat{N})$ be the allocatable inputs, for example, labor and energy.

In this case we may estimate the aggregate industry 'output' under constant returns to scale as the solution to the following linear programming problem

$$\vec{D}_o^M(x_{11}, \ldots, x_{1\hat{N}}, \ldots, x_{K1}, \ldots, x_{K\hat{N}}, \sum_{k=1}^{K} x_{\hat{N}+1}^k, \ldots, \sum_{k=1}^{K} x_N^k, \sum_{k=1}^{K} y^k; 1) \tag{3.59}$$

$= \max \sum_{k=1}^K \beta_k$

s.t.

$$
\begin{array}{llll}
(Firm\ 1) & \sum_{k=1}^K z_k^1 y_{km} \geqq y_{1m} + \beta_1, & m = 1, \ldots, M \\
& \sum_{k=1}^K z_k^1 x_{kn} \leqq x_{1n}, & n = 1, \ldots, \hat{N} \\
& \sum_{k=1}^K z_k^1 x_{kn} \leqq x_{1n}, & n = \hat{N}+1, \ldots, N \\
& z_k^1 \geqq 0, k = 1, \ldots, K. & \\
& \vdots & \\
(Firm\ K) & \sum_{k=1}^K z_k^K y_{km} \geqq y_{Km} + \beta_K, & m = 1, \ldots, M \\
& \sum_{k=1}^K z_k^K x_{kn} \leqq x_{Kn}, & n = 1, \ldots, \hat{N} \\
& \sum_{k=1}^K z_k^K x_{kn} \leqq x_{Kn}, & n = \hat{N}+1, \ldots, N \\
& z_k^K \geqq 0, k = 1, \ldots, K. & \\
(Summation) & \sum_{k=1}^K x_{kn} \leqq x_n, & n = \hat{N}+1, \ldots, N.
\end{array}
$$

Notice that the dimensionality of this problem is much larger than earlier formulations in this essay. Specifically, there is a separate vector of intensity variables for each firm, which is required to allow for the different fixed inputs associated with each observation. Also, in contrast to the standard technical efficiency measure problems, we solve one aggregate problem rather than K individual firm or observation problems.

5. Aggregating Farrell Efficiency Indexes

This section develops techniques for aggregating the output and input oriented Farrell efficiency indexes. These efficiency measures are the type which generated the Fox paradox, i.e., the individual efficiency measures are in ratio form, which is not consistent with simple additive aggregation. As we show in this section, if we maintain the ratio form for the efficiency measures, consistent aggregation requires more structure, in particular, we need to use the traditional aggregation technique of value share-weighting. This means that when we aggregate technical efficiency measures, they will no longer be independent of prices, since these are required to construct the shares.

Beginning with the output oriented case, recall that revenue efficiency is the ratio of maximal to observed revenue and that the industry revenue function is the sum of the firm revenue functions. With these two observations at hand we may construct industry efficiency as a share weighted aggregate of firm efficiencies. Since

$$R(x^1,\ldots,x^K,p) = \sum_{k=1}^{K} R^k(x^k,p), \tag{3.60}$$

we obtain

$$\frac{R(x^1,\ldots,x^K,p)}{p\sum_{k=1}^{K} y^k} = \sum_{k=1}^{K} \frac{R^k(x^k,p)}{py^k} s_o^k, \tag{3.61}$$

where $s_o^k = py^k/(p\sum_{k=1}^{K} y^k)$ is firm $k's$ share of the total observed value of outputs, thus it is nonnegative and $\sum_{k=1}^{K} s_o^k = 1$. As usual, observed industry output is the sum of the firm outputs,

$$y = \sum_{k=1}^{K} y^k. \tag{3.62}$$

We formulate the Blackorby and Russell (1999) aggregate indication axiom for this case in the following way. The industry is considered to be efficient if and only if each of its firms is efficient, i.e.,

$$\frac{R(x^1,\ldots,x^K,p)}{p\sum_{k=1}^K y^k} = 1 \text{ if and only if } \frac{R^k(x^k,p)}{py^k} = 1, k=1,\ldots,K.$$

We note that this follows for this case since each firm efficiency index is greater than or equal to one.

Since Farrell revenue efficiency may be decomposed multiplicatively into a technical and allocative component, we turn to aggregation of the components. Since we know that $R(x,p)/py = FA_o/D_o(x,y)$ we find that

$$\frac{FA_o}{D_o(x^1,\ldots,x^K,\sum_{k=1}^K y^k)} = \sum_{k=1}^K \frac{FA_o^k}{D_o^k(x^k,y^k)} s_o^k, \tag{3.63}$$

where the industry output distance function is defined as

$$D_o(x^1,\ldots,x^K,\sum_{k=1}^K y^k) = \max\{\theta : \sum_{k=1}^K y^k/\theta \in P(x^1,\ldots,x^K)\}. \tag{3.64}$$

If each firm is as allocatively efficient as the industry, i.e., if $FA_o = FA_o^k$ for all $k=1,\ldots,K$, then it follows from (3.63) that

$$\begin{aligned}\frac{1}{D_o(x^1,\ldots,x^k,\sum_{k=1}^K y^k)} &= F_o(x^1,\ldots,x^K,\sum_{k=1}^K y^k) \qquad (3.65)\\ = \sum_{k=1}^K F_o^k(x^k,y^k)s_o^k &= \sum_{k=1}^K \frac{s_o^k}{D_o^k(x^k,y^k)}\end{aligned}$$

In words, the Farrell industry index of technical efficiency equals the share-weighted sum of the firm indexes.

We note that the aggregation of technical efficiency indexes is in some respects more demanding than the aggregation of technical efficiency indicators. In both cases we have assumed some form of allocative efficiency to simplify the expression, however, in the index case, we still require a price related term—namely the share—to accomplish aggregation.

If we assume that a single output is produced, matters are simpler: first, there is no allocative inefficiency so our assumption is automatically satisfied. Second the shares become price independent, i.e.,

$$s_o^k = \frac{py^k}{p\sum_{k=1}^K y^k} = \frac{y^k}{\sum_{k=1}^K y^k}. \tag{3.66}$$

Thus in the single output case, the aggregation of output oriented Farrell Indexes simplifies to

$$\begin{aligned}\frac{R(x^1,\ldots,x^K,p)}{p\sum_{k=1}^K y^k} &= F_o(x^1,\ldots,x^K,\sum_{k=1}^K y^k) \\ &= \sum_{k=1}^K F_o^k(x^k,y^k)\frac{y^k}{\sum_{k=1}^K y^k} \\ &= \sum_{k=1}^K \frac{R^k(x^k,p)}{py^k}\frac{y^k}{\sum_{k=1}^K y^k}.\end{aligned} \tag{3.67}$$

If we wish to find price independent weights for aggregation in the multiple output case, one possible candidate is the following generalization of the single output case

$$\frac{1}{M}(\sum_{m=1}^M \frac{y_{km}}{\sum_{k=1}^K y_{km}}), k = 1,\ldots,K.$$

These weights are the average of each firm's share of each of the M outputs.

Finally, if we wish to relax the assumption that each firm has the same allocative efficiency, we may follow Li and Ng (1995) and define industry allocative efficiency as

$$FA_o = \sum_{k=1}^K FA_o^k \cdot \hat{s}_o^k,$$

where the firm allocative efficiency FA_o^k is defined as a residual, i.e.,

$$FA_o^k = D_o^k(x^k,y^k)\frac{R^k(x^k,p)}{py^k},$$

but the weights are now defined

$$\hat{s}_o^k = \frac{p(y^k/D_o^k(x^k,y^k))}{p\sum_{k=1}^K(y^k/D_o^k(x^k,y^k))}.$$

These weights differ from those defined earlier in that they are based on potential outputs $y^k/D_o^k(x^k, y^k)$ rather than observed outputs y^k.

Using these weights we may decompose the industry revenue index into a technical and allocative component as follows

$$\frac{R(x^1,\ldots,x^K,p)}{p\sum_{k=1}^K y^k} = (\sum_{k=1}^K F_o^k(x^k,y^k)\hat{s}_o^k)FA_o.$$

Next we turn to aggregation of the Farrell cost efficiency index. Since this closely parallels what we have for the revenue efficiency index, we focus on the essentials. Recall that the cost indexes are ratios of minimum and observed cost, and that industry costs are the simple sum of firm costs. This allows us to write

$$\frac{C(y^1,\ldots,y^K,w)}{w\sum_{k=1}^K x^k} = \sum_{k=1}^K \frac{C^k(y^k,w)}{wx^k}s_i^k, \tag{3.68}$$

where the left-hand-side is the industry cost efficiency index and the right-hand-side is the share-weighted sum of the associated firm indexes. Thus the Farrell industry index of cost efficiency is obtained by adding up the individual share-weighted firm Farrell indexes of cost efficiency. The cost shares are defined as $s_i^k = wx^k/(w\sum_{k=1}^K x^k)$ and are nonnegative and sum to one.

If there is no (input) allocative inefficiency, then the industry index of technical efficiency is derived as the share-weighted sum of the firm indexes, i.e.,

$$F_i(y^1,\ldots,y^K,\sum_{k=1}^K x^k) = \sum_{k=1}^K F_i^k(y^k,x^k)s_i^k, \tag{3.69}$$

where $F_i(y^1,\ldots,y^K,\sum_{k=1}^K x^k)$ is the Farrell index of technical efficiency defined on the industry input set, i.e.,

$$F_i(y^1,\ldots,y^K,\sum_{k=1}^K x^k) = \min\{\lambda : \sum_{k=1}^K x^k/\lambda \in L(y^1,\ldots,y^K)\}. \tag{3.70}$$

As we did for the revenue indexes we define our industry allocative efficiency scores as the share weighted firm scores

$$AE_i = \sum_{k=1}^{K} AE_i^k \hat{s}_i^k,$$

where these weights are defined as

$$\hat{s}_i^k = \frac{w(x^k/D_i^k(y^k,x^k))}{w\sum_{k=1}^{K}(x^k/D_i^k(y^k,x^k))}.$$

Now we have the following decomposition of the industry cost efficiency index

$$\frac{C(y^1,\ldots,y^K,w)}{w\sum_{k=1}^{K}x^k} = (\sum_{k=1}^{K} F_i^k(y^k,x^k)\cdot\hat{s}_i^k)AE_i,$$

which has the usual interpretation.

6. The Luenberger Firm and Industry Productivity Indicators

This section discusses the Luenberger productivity indicator, its dual and its decomposition. As in the rest of this chapter, we emphasize issues of aggregation.

Recall that the Luenberger productivity indicator for technologies T^t and T^{t+1} takes the form

$$\begin{aligned}\pounds(x^t,y^t,x^{t+1},y^{t+1};g_x g_y) &= 1/2[\vec{D}_T^{t+1}(x^t,y^t;g_x,g_y) \\ &- \vec{D}_T^{t+1}(x^{t+1},y^{t+1};g_x,g_y) + \vec{D}_T^t(x^t,y^t;g_x,g_y) \\ &- \vec{D}_T^t(x^{t+1},y^{t+1};g_x,g_y)].\end{aligned} \tag{3.71}$$

Again if we appeal to the assumption of no allocative inefficiency, then the industry directional technology distance function is exactly equal to the sum of its firm distance functions,

$$\vec{D}_T(\sum_{k=1}^{K}x^k,\sum_{k=1}^{K}y^k;g_x,g_y) = \sum_{k=1}^{K}\vec{D}_{T^k}(x^k,y^k;g_x,g_y) \tag{3.72}$$

From this observation it follows that the 'primal' Luenberger productivity indicator aggregates. That is, we have

$$\begin{aligned} &£\left(\sum_{k=1}^{K} x^{k,t}, \sum_{k=1}^{K} y^{k,t}, \sum_{k=1}^{K} x^{k,t+1}, \sum_{k=1}^{K} y^{k,t+1}; g_x, g_y\right) \\ &= \sum_{k=1}^{K} £^k(x^{k,t}, y^{k,t}, x^{k,t+1}, y^{k,t+1}; g_x, g_y), \end{aligned} \tag{3.73}$$

where

$$\begin{aligned} £^k(x^{k,t}, y^{k,t}, x^{k,t+1}, y^{k,t+1}; g_x, g_y) &= \\ & 1/2[\vec{D}_{T^k}^{t+1}(x^{k,t}, y^{k,t}; g_x, g_y) \\ &- \vec{D}_{T^k}^{t+1}(x^{k,t+1}, y^{k,t+1}; g_x, g_y) \\ &+ \vec{D}_{T^k}^{t}(x^{k,t}, y^{k,t}; g_x, g_y) \\ &- \vec{D}_{T^k}^{t}(x^{k,t+1}, y^{k,t+1}; g_x, g_y)], \end{aligned} \tag{3.74}$$

is firm $k's$ Luenberger productivity indicator.

Note that by appropriately choosing the directional vectors one may aggregate any directional distance function, including those used to incorporate undesirable outputs (see Essay 2).

7. Aggregation Across Inputs and Outputs

In some situations it may not be possible to obtain data on input and output quantities; instead, data are available in value terms, for example revenues and costs. In this section we address that issue by introducing models which use input and output prices to aggregate inputs and outputs, respectively, which as byproducts provide us with conditions under which revenue and cost data may be used in place of output and input quantities. We also show how both types of data may be incorporated into our efficiency models.

We restrict our analysis to the activity analysis model and focus on aggregation of technical efficiency measures, i.e., we derive conditions under which price aggregation does not affect the value of our technical efficiency measures. We begin with a numerical example as motivation, and then turn to a more formal presentation of the problem for both

Farrell technical efficiency indexes as well as our technical efficiency indicators.

To illustrate our problem, consider three firms, $k = 1, 2, 3$ using two inputs (x_{k1}, x_{k2}) to produce a single output y_k. Let the values of the inputs and outputs be given by

Table 3.1 Firm Data

	Firm		
	1	*2*	*3*
y	1	1	1
x_1	1	2	3
x_2	2	1	3/2
c	5	4	6
$F_i(y, x)$	1	1	2/3
$AF_i(y, c)$	4/5	1	2/3
$C(y, w)/c$	4/5	1	2/3
$FA_i(y, x, w)$	4/5	1	1

In addition let the prices of inputs be such that $w_1 = 1$ and $w_2 = 2$ for all three firms. Then we may aggregate inputs into costs as

$$w_1 x_{k1} + w_2 x_{k2} = c_k.$$

Each firm's input cost is that associated with the fourth row in Table 3.1.

We are interested in learning when the input-oriented measure of technical efficiency based on quantity data yields the same score when based on the cost aggregated data. Specifically, when is the solution to

$$\begin{aligned} F_i(y^{k'}, x^{k'}) &= \min \lambda \qquad (3.75) \\ & s.t. \sum_{k=1}^{K} z_k y_{km} \geqq y_{k'm}, m = 1, \ldots, M \\ & \sum_{k=1}^{K} z_k x_{kn} \leqq \lambda x_{k'n}, n = 1, \ldots, N \\ & z_k \geqq 0, k = 1, \ldots, K \end{aligned}$$

the same as the solution to

$$
\begin{aligned}
AF_i(y^{k'}, c^{k'}) \quad &= \quad \min \lambda && (3.76)\\
s.t. \quad &\sum_{k=1}^{K} z_k y_{km} \geqq y_{k'}, m = 1, \ldots, M\\
&\sum_{k=1}^{K} z_k c_k \leqq \lambda c_{k'}\\
&z_k \geqq 0, k = 1, \ldots, K.
\end{aligned}
$$

In our simple example above, we can see that the solution value is the same for observations 2 and 3, but that is not the case for observation 1, see rows 5 and 6 in Table 3.1. To find conditions under which our two problems yield the same efficiency scores, first consider the traditional cost minimization problem

$$
\begin{aligned}
C(y^{k'}, w) \quad &= \quad \min \sum_{n=1}^{N} w_n x_n && (3.77)\\
s.t. \quad &\sum_{k=1}^{K} z_k y_{km} \geqq y_{k'm}, m = 1, \ldots, M,\\
&\sum_{k=1}^{K} z_k x_{kn} \leqq x_n, n = 1, \ldots, N,\\
&z_k \geqq 0, k = 1, \ldots, K.
\end{aligned}
$$

We may state the following Lemma.

Lemma : Let $w_n > 0, n = 1, \ldots, N$, then $C(y^{k'}, w) = AF_i(y^{k'}, c^{k'})c_{k'}$.

Recall from Essay 1 that the Farrell index of cost efficiency may be written as

$$FC(y, x, w) = \frac{C(y, w)}{wx} = F_i(y, x)FA_i(y, x, w).$$

Thus by the Lemma above we have

$$F_i(y, x) = AF_i(y, c), \tag{3.78}$$

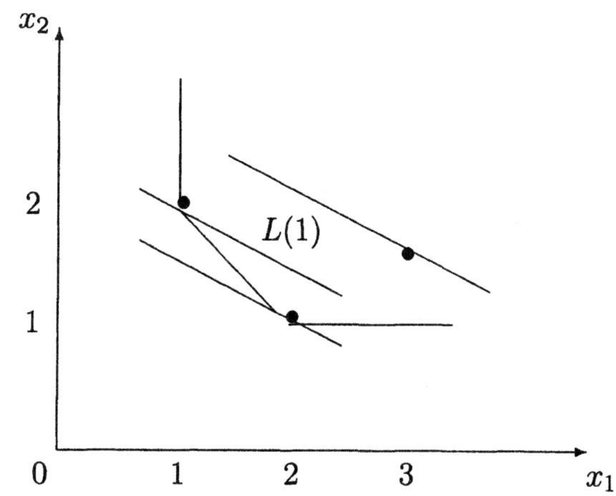

Figure 3.4. Input Aggregation

if and only if $FA_i(y, x, w) = 1$. In words, Farrell input oriented technical efficiency will equal the cost aggregated efficiency score if and only if the input vector x is allocatively efficient.[2] This is confirmed by the data in Table 3.1; $F_i(y, x)$ and $AF_i(y, c)$ agree only when $FA_i(y, x, w) = 1$. Figure 3.4 corroborates this result.

What does it mean for x to be allocatively efficient? To see this, let x^* be the optimizer in the cost minimization problem above, so that

$$C(y, w) = wx^*.$$

Then from the decomposition of the Farrell cost efficiency index, imposing allocative efficiency implies setting $FA_i(y, x, w) = 1$, which yields

$$wx^* = F_i(y, x)wx.$$

Thus if $w_n > 0, n = 1, \ldots, N$, then if x is allocatively efficient, it means that

$$x_n^* = F_i(y, x) \cdot x_n, n = 1, \ldots, N,$$

[2]Recall that we have also assumed that all observations face the same price for each input.

i.e., the cost minimizers x_n^* are radial contractions of the observed inputs $x_n, n = 1, \ldots, N$.

We now turn to a more general and formal presentation of the problem. As usual there are $k = 1, \ldots, K$ observations of inputs $x^k \in \Re_+^N$ and outputs $y^k \in \Re_+^M$. We begin with cost aggregation. Therefore we need input prices $w \in \Re_+^N$, and assume that each firm faces the same vector of prices w.

We define (cost) aggregate input as

$$c_{k\hat{N}} = \sum_{n=1}^{\hat{N}} w_n x_{kn}, k = 1, \ldots, K, \hat{N} \leqq N.$$

The input $c_{k\hat{N}}$ is the value or cost of the first $n = 1, \ldots, \hat{N}$ inputs. If $\hat{N} = N$ then all inputs are aggregated into one variable.

Next we introduce the idea of unbiased input aggregation in terms of Farrell technical efficiency. Thus define the input oriented **Farrell Subvector Index of Technical Efficiency**

$$\begin{aligned} SF_i(y^{k'}, x^{k'}) &= \min \lambda \\ s.t. \ \textstyle\sum_{k=1}^K z_k y_{km} &\geqq y_{k'm}, m = 1, \ldots, M, \\ \textstyle\sum_{k=1}^K z_k x_{kn} &\leqq \lambda x_{k'n}, n = 1, \ldots, \hat{N}, \\ \textstyle\sum_{k=1}^K z_k x_{kn} &\leqq x_{k'n}, n = \hat{N}+1, \ldots, N, \\ z_k \geqq 0, & \quad k = 1, \ldots, K. \end{aligned}$$

This linear programming problem differs from the standard constant returns to scale measure of technical efficiency in that we scale only on the first $n = 1, \ldots, \hat{N}$ inputs, hence the name subvector efficiency.

To define what we mean by unbiased aggregation define the **Aggregate Farrell Input Index of Technical Efficiency** as

$$\begin{aligned} AF_i(y^{k'}, c_{k'\hat{N}}, x_{k'\hat{N}+1}, \ldots, x_{k'N}) &= \min \lambda \\ s.t. \sum_{k=1}^K z_k y_{km} \geqq y_{k'm}, \quad & m = 1, \ldots, M, \end{aligned}$$

$$\sum_{k=1}^{K} z_k c_{k\hat{N}} \leqq \lambda c_{k'\hat{N}},$$
$$\sum_{k=1}^{K} z_k x_{kn} \leqq x_{k'n}, \qquad n = \hat{N}+1,\ldots,N,$$
$$z_k \geqq 0, \qquad k = 1,\ldots,K.$$

In this problem the first $n = 1,\ldots,\hat{N}$ inputs have been aggregated into one variable, therefore this problem has $(\hat{N}-1)$ fewer constraints than the subvector problem SF_i.

We say that **Input Aggregation is (Farrell) Index Unbiased** if and only if

$$SF_i(y^{k'}, x^{k'}) = AF_i(y^{k'}, c_{k'\hat{N}}, x_{k'\hat{N}+1},\ldots,x_{k'N}).$$

Thus what we mean by unbiased is that we may use cost data rather than input quantities when we compute the Farrell input oriented index of technical efficiency.

To establish the conditions under which the aggregation is unbiased we define the **Subvector (or short run) Cost Function** as

$$\begin{aligned} C(y^{k'}, w_1,\ldots,w_{\hat{N}}, x_{k'\hat{N}+1},\ldots,x_{k'N}) &= \min \sum_{n=1}^{\hat{N}} w_n x_n \\ s.t. \sum_{k=1}^{K} z_k y_{km} &\geqq y_{k'm}, m = 1,\ldots,M, \\ \sum_{k=1}^{K} z_k x_{kn} &\leqq x_n, n = 1,\ldots,\hat{N}, \\ \sum_{k=1}^{K} z_k x_{kn} &\leqq x_{k'n}, n = \hat{N}+1,\ldots,N, \\ z_k &\geqq 0, \ k = 1,\ldots,K. \end{aligned}$$

We use this cost function to define a subvector variation of Farrell's cost efficiency index,

$$C(y^{k'}, w_1,\ldots,w_{\hat{N}}, x_{k'\hat{N}+1},\ldots,x_{k'N})/c_{k'\hat{N}} = SF_i(y^{k'}, x^{k'}) \cdot SAE_i,$$

where SAE_i is a **Subvector Input Allocative Efficiency** residual. Thus the subvector index has the same decomposition properties as the standard Farrell approach.

If $w_n > 0, n = 1.\ldots, \hat{N}$, then

$$\begin{aligned} & C(y^{k'}, w_1, \ldots, w_{\hat{N}}, x_{k'\hat{N}+1}, \ldots, x_{k'N})/c_{k'\hat{N}} \\ &= AF_i(y^{k'}, c_{k'\hat{N}}, x_{k'\hat{N}+1}, \ldots, x_{k'N}), \end{aligned}$$

thus it follows from our definition of unbiasedness and the decomposition of our subvector cost efficiency measure that input aggregation is unbiased if and only if $SAE_i = 1$, i.e., if and only if there is no subvector allocative inefficiency. If it turns out that there is allocative inefficiency, i.e., $SAE_i < 1$, then the aggregated efficiency measure is bounded from above by the subvector technical efficiency index, i.e.,

$$AF_i(y^{k'}, c_{k'\hat{N}}, x_{k'\hat{N}+1}, \ldots, x_{k'N}) \leqq SF_i(y^{k'}, x^{k'}).$$

Again this follows from our aggregation condition and the subvector cost efficiency decomposition.

In order to find conditions for unbiased input aggregation for the input *indicator*, we first introduce a **Subvector Directional Input Distance Function**, where $g_x = (g_{x_1}, \ldots, g_{x_{\hat{N}}})$ as

$$\begin{aligned} S\vec{D}_i(y^{k'}, x^{k'}; g_x) \quad &= \max \beta \\ s.t. \ \textstyle\sum_{k=1}^{K} z_k y_{km} \quad &\geqq y_{k'm}, m = 1, \ldots, M, \\ \textstyle\sum_{k=1}^{K} z_k x_{kn} \quad &\leqq x_{k'n} - \beta g_{x_n}, n = 1, \ldots, \hat{N}, \\ \textstyle\sum_{k=1}^{K} z_k x_{kn} \quad &\leqq x_{k'n}, n = \hat{N}+1, \ldots, N, \\ z_k \geqq 0, \quad & k = 1, \ldots, K. \end{aligned}$$

In contrast to the input directional distance function from Essay 1, the above function translates only on the first $n = 1, \ldots, \hat{N}$ inputs. Of course if $\hat{N} = N$, we are back to the standard directional distance function.

Following the procedure we used for the Farrell index, we next introduce the **Cost Aggregated Directional Input Distance Function** as

$$\begin{aligned}
\vec{AD}_i(y^{k'}, c_{k'\hat{N}}, x_{k'\hat{N}+1}, \ldots, x_{k'N}; \sum_{n=1}^{\hat{N}} w_n g_{x_n}) &= \max \beta \\
s.t. \sum_{k=1}^{K} z_k y_{km} \geqq y_{k'm}, &\qquad m = 1, \ldots, M, \\
\sum_{k=1}^{K} z_k c_{k\hat{N}} \leqq c_{k'\hat{N}} - \beta \sum_{n=1}^{\hat{N}} w_n g_{x_n}, & \\
\sum_{k=1}^{K} z_k x_{kn} \leqq x_{k'n}, &\qquad n = \hat{N}+1, \ldots, N, \\
z_k \geqq 0, &\qquad k = 1, \ldots, K.
\end{aligned}$$

Note that in this problem the β is scaling on the *value* of the directional vector rather than the directional vector alone. We say that input aggregation is indicator unbiased if and only if

$$\begin{aligned}
&\vec{SD}_i(y^{k'}, x^{k'}; g_x) \\
&= \vec{AD}_i(y^{k'}, c_{k'\hat{N}}, x_{k'\hat{N}+1}, \ldots, x_{k'N}; \sum_{n=1}^{\hat{N}} w_n g_{x_n}).
\end{aligned}$$

Unbiasedness in this case means that cost data rather than input data may be used in the calculation of the (subvector) technical indicator without changing the solution value.

To find conditions required for unbiased aggregation of the input indicator, we introduce a **Subvector (short run) Cost Efficiency Indicator**, modified from Essay 1 as

$$\begin{aligned}
&SCI(y^{k'}, c_{k'\hat{N}}, x_{k'\hat{N}+1}, \ldots, x_{k'N}; g_x) = \\
&\frac{c_{k'n} - C(y^{k'}, w_1, \ldots, w_{\hat{N}}, x_{k'\hat{N}+1}, \ldots, x_{k'N})}{\sum_{n=1}^{\hat{N}} w_n g_{x_n}},
\end{aligned}$$

with its decomposition into technical and allocative efficiency

$$SCI(y^{k'}, c_{k'\hat{N}}, x_{k'\hat{N}+1}, \ldots, x_{k'N}; g_x) = \vec{SD}_i(y^{k'}, x^{k'}; g_x) + S\vec{AE}_i.$$

From the decomposition of the subvector cost indicator, it is clear that our condition for unbiased aggregation will be satisfied if and only if $\vec{SAE_i} = 0$, i.e., there is no allocative inefficiency. Moreover, if $\vec{SAE_i} > 0$, then the aggregate measure is bounded from above by the subvector technical efficiency indicator, i.e.,

$$\vec{AD_i}(y^{k'}, c_{k'\hat{N}}, x_{k'\hat{N}+1}, \ldots, x_{k'N}; \sum_{n=1}^{\hat{N}} w_n g_{x_n}) \leqq \vec{SD_i}(y^{k'}, x^{k'}; g_x),$$

It is obvious at this point that the input aggregation schemes have analogs on the output side. Again allocative efficiencies play a key role for unbiased aggregation. With this in mind the rest of this section will be brief.

We define an aggregated output as

$$r_{k\hat{M}} = \sum_{m=1}^{\hat{M}} p_m y_{km}, k = 1, \ldots, K, \hat{M} \leqq M.$$

The output $r_{k\hat{M}}$ is firm k's revenue from its first $m = 1, \ldots, \hat{M}$ outputs. We assume that each firm $k = 1, \ldots, K$ faces the same output prices, $p_m, m = 1, \ldots, \hat{M}$.

As in the case for inputs we say that the aggregation of outputs is unbiased when the output oriented Farrell index of technical efficiency is equal to the aggregate measure. To formalize this statement, we first introduce the **Farrell Output Subvector Index of Technical Efficiency** as

$$\begin{aligned} SF_o(x^{k'}, y^{k'}) &= \max \theta \\ s.t. \quad & \sum_{k=1}^{K} z_k y_{km} \geqq \theta y_{k'm}, m = 1, \ldots, \hat{M} \\ & \sum_{k=1}^{K} z_k y_{km} \geqq y_{k'm}, m = \hat{M}+1, \ldots, M, \\ & \sum_{k=1}^{K} z_k x_{kn} \leqq x_{k'n}, n = 1, \ldots, N, \\ & z_k \geqq 0, k = 1, \ldots, K. \end{aligned}$$

The next linear programming problem is the **Revenue Aggregate Farrell Output Index of Technical Efficiency**, in which the first $\hat{M}$ outputs are aggregated into their associated level of revenue

$$\begin{aligned} AF_o(x^{k'}, r_{k'\hat{M}}, y_{k'\hat{M}+1}, \ldots, y_{k'M}) &= \max \theta \\ s.t. \sum_{k=1}^{K} z_k r_{k\hat{M}} &\geqq \theta r_{k'\hat{M}}, \\ \sum_{k=1}^{K} z_k y_{km} &\geqq y_{k'm}, \quad m = \hat{M}+1, \ldots, M, \\ \sum_{k=1}^{K} z_k x_{kn} &\leqq x_{k'n}, \quad n = 1, \ldots, N, \\ z_k &\geqq 0, \quad k = 1, \ldots, K. \end{aligned}$$

We say that output aggregation is (Farrell) index unbiased if and only if

$$SF_o(x^{k'}, y^{k'}) = AF_o(x^{k'}, r_{k'\hat{M}}, y_{k'\hat{M}+1}, \ldots, y_{k'M}).$$

In words this means that we may use revenue data in place of data on individual output quantities in calculating Farrell output technical efficiency.

The logic from the input side may be applied to prove that output aggregation is Farrell index unbiased if and only if there is no output (subvector) allocative inefficiency. Moreover, if there is such inefficiency, the aggregate measure is bounded below by the technical (sub)index. Formally,

$$SF_o(x^{k'}, y^{k'}) \leqq AF_o(x^{k'}, r_{k'\hat{M}}, y_{k'\hat{M}+1}, \ldots, y_{k'M}).$$

This result follows from the fact that the output index of allocative efficiency is greater than or equal to one. Note that in the case of the input oriented measures, the inequality on the bound is reversed since input allocative efficiency is less than or equal to one.

Turning to the case of indicators, the two linear programming problems that are required to analyze whether output aggregation is unbiased are the aggregated directional output distance function and the corresponding subvector function. Formally,

$$\begin{aligned} A\vec{D}_o(x^{k'}, r_{k'\hat{M}}, y_{k'\hat{M}+1}, \ldots, y_{k'M}; \sum_{m=1}^{\hat{M}} p_m g_{y_m}) &= \max \beta \\ s.t. \sum_{k=1}^{K} z_k r_{k\hat{M}} \geqq r_{k'\hat{M}} + \beta \sum_{m=1}^{\hat{M}} p_m g_{y_m}, & \\ \sum_{k=1}^{K} z_k y_{km} \geqq y_{k'm}, & \quad m = \hat{M}+1, \ldots, M, \\ \sum_{k=1}^{K} z_k x_{kn} \leqq x_{k'n}, & \quad n = 1, \ldots, N, \\ z_k \geqq 0, & \quad k = 1, \ldots, K, \end{aligned}$$

where $g_y = (g_{y_1}, \ldots, g_{y_{\hat{M}}})$ and

$$\begin{aligned} S\vec{D}_o(x^{k'}, y^{k'}; g_y) &= \max \beta \\ s.t. \quad & \sum_{k=1}^{K} z_k y_{km} \geqq y^{k'} + \beta g_{y_m}, m = 1, \ldots, \hat{M} \\ & \sum_{k=1}^{K} z_k y_{km} \geqq y_{k'm}, m = \hat{M}+1, \ldots, M, \\ & \sum_{k=1}^{K} z_k x_{kn} \leqq x_{k'n}, n = 1, \ldots, N, \\ & z_k \geqq 0, k = 1, \ldots, K, \end{aligned}$$

respectively.

We say that output aggregation is indicator unbiased if and only if

$$S\vec{D}_o(x^{k'}, y^{k'}; g_y) = A\vec{D}_o(x^{k'}, r_{k'\hat{M}}, y_{k'\hat{M}+1}, \ldots, y_{k'M}; \sum_{m=1}^{\hat{M}} p_m g_{y_m}).$$

If aggregation is unbiased, we may use revenue data to compute the output oriented indicator without affecting the resulting measure of technical efficiency. This holds if and only if there is no associated allocative inefficiency. As before, in the presence of allocative inefficiency aggregation is biased, but we may establish the bound as

$$S\vec{D}_o(x^{k'}, y^{k'}; g_y) \geqq A\vec{D}_o(x^{k'}, r_{k'\hat{M}}, y_{k'\hat{M}+1}, \ldots, y_{k'M}; \sum_{m=1}^{\hat{M}} p_m g_{y_m}),$$

i.e., the aggregate indicator is bounded from above by the subvector directional output distance function.

Throughout this section we have assumed that our technology exhibits constant returns to scale and that inputs and outputs are freely disposable. The aggregation results hold, however, even if we allow for variable returns to scale and weak disposability of inputs or outputs.

8. Aggregation and Decompositions

From Essay 1 we recall that the Farrell cost and revenue indexes decompose into technical and allocative components, respectively. These decompositions are multiplicative. Earlier in this Essay we showed that one may aggregate the Farrell indexes by introducing weights. We note, however, that two types of weights are required, which is the issue we address in this section.

We start by assuming that the aggregate industry indexes should mimic the firm decompositions in that they should be multiplicative. We then ask what implications imposing this structure has on the way in which the components must be aggregated. In essence we are reversing the arguments raised in the section on the Fox Paradox. There we took the form of the aggregation as given and asked what the associated implications were for the form of the disaggregated index.

We show that a weighted geometric mean is required to maintain a multiplicative decomposition of the aggregated indexes. We then show how to choose the weights; by approximation we show that cost and revenue weights may be used.

To avoid unnecessary repetition we use the following notation; r_k is firm $k's$ allocative efficiency component and s_k refers to its technical efficiency component. The product of these $q_k = r_k s_k$ is its overall index, which could be either a cost or revenue efficiency index. For simplicity we assume that $k = 1, 2$.

We assume that the industry or aggregate index preserves the multiplicative structure of the decomposition so that

$$\Delta(q_1, q_2) = \Delta(r_1, r_2)\Delta(s_1, s_2), \tag{3.79}$$

where Δ is a continuous real-valued function that aggregates the firm indexes into industry indexes. It follows from Aczél (1990, p.27) that the solution to the above functional equation is

$$\Delta(t_1, t_2) = t_1^{\alpha_1} t_2^{\alpha_2}, \tag{3.80}$$

where α_1 and α_2 are arbitrary constants. Applying (3.80) to (3.79) we find that

$$(q_1^{\alpha_1} q_2^{\alpha_2}) = [(r_1^{\alpha_1} r_2^{\alpha_2})(s_1^{\alpha_1} s_2^{\alpha_2})], \tag{3.81}$$

where the bracketed expressions are the aggregates, i.e., the industry indexes.

We may think of the expression above as starting from the decompositions at the firm level,

$$q_k = r_k s_k, k = 1, 2 \tag{3.82}$$

where we then impose the geometric weights $\alpha_k, k = 1, 2$ and multiply them together

$$(q_1^{\alpha_1})(q_2^{\alpha_2}) = (r_1 s_1)^{\alpha_1} (r_2 s_2)^{\alpha_2}, \tag{3.83}$$

which gives us (3.81).

Our next task is to find the appropriate form of the weights $\alpha_k, k = 1, 2$. For this we start by approximating (3.80) around $t_1 = t_2 = 1$, and assuming that $\alpha_1 + \alpha_2 = 1$,

$$\begin{aligned} \Delta(t_1, t_2) &= 1^{\alpha_1} 1^{\alpha_2} + \alpha_1 (1^{\alpha_1 - 1} 1^{\alpha_2})(t_1 - 1) \\ &+ \alpha_2 (1^{\alpha_1} 1^{\alpha_2 - 1})(t_2 - 1) \\ &= \alpha_1 t_1 + \alpha_2 t_2. \end{aligned} \tag{3.84}$$

In section 5 of this Essay we showed that the industry revenue efficiency index was the share weighted sum of the firm indexes, i.e, in our case with $k = 1, 2$

$$\frac{R(x^1, x^2; p)}{p(y^1 + y^2)} = \frac{R(x^1, p)}{py^1} s_o^1 + \frac{R(x^2, p)}{py^2} s_o^2. \tag{3.85}$$

Thus if we set our approximation to be consistent with (3.84) then our unknown weight α_k must be taken to be equal to our output share s_o^k. Hence if our first order approximation is acceptable, shares may be used in the aggregation of the Farrell revenue efficiency index while preserving the multiplicative decomposition.

Similar arguments may be applied to the cost side; input shares may be used to preserve the multiplicative decomposition of cost efficiency at the industry level.

Next we turn to an application.

9. Efficiency and Profitability in the Japanese Banking Industry

by

Hirofumi Fukuyama and William L. Weber

9.1 Introduction

In recent years capital markets have become increasingly global in scope during a period of financial market deregulation. Berger and Humphrey (1997) review the numerous studies that estimate the efficiency and productivity change of individual financial institutions. However, inferring industry efficiency from average firm efficiency can be problematic. (Blackorby and Russell 1999, Ylvinger 2000) To the extent that policymakers use estimates of firm efficiency to evaluate the effects of deregulation and other policy changes, a lack of consistent aggregates of industry efficiency can have serious consequences. In this paper we estimate aggregate efficiency and profitability change for the Japanese banking industry for the period 1992-1996. Linear programming (Data Envelopment Analysis-DEA) methods are used to estimate the maximal profit function and the directional technology distance function. We find evidence that industry profit efficiency declines during 1992-1996 and that bank profit inefficiency is least among city banks and greatest for regional banks. In the next section we briefly review events which had an impact on the Japanese banking industry and the Japanese economy. Following this review we present the directional technology distance function and the maximal profit function in a DEA framework so that the Nerlovian profit efficiency indicator and the Luenberger profitability change indicator can be estimated and aggregated to the industry level. We then describe the data and present the empirical results. The last section is a summary of our work.

9.2 The Japanese Banking System

While the Japanese money supply experienced double digit growth during the 1980s consumer price inflation was relatively mild, cresting at 3.3% in 1991. Instead, the monetary expansion helped fuel real estate and security price inflation. The Nikkei stock index reached its apex of 38,916 at the end of 1989. In 1990 the bubble burst with stock prices falling more than 50 percent by 1992 and going below 13,000 in 1998. Similarly, land prices in the late 1990s were only 25 percent of their peaks. The bursting of the bubble hit Japanese banks particularly hard. In the 1980s, lacking strong loan demand from manufacturing, Japanese banks increased their lending to the real estate, construction, and the non-bank financial sectors. Land served as the primary source of capital (see Mattione 2000). When the bubble burst, banks were left with bad loans estimated to be as high 16 percent of GDP. The run-up in stock and real estate prices also served to increase Japanese bank size. In 1972 the US was home to nine of the ten largest banks in the world but by 1992 Japan claimed eight of the ten largest banks in the world. Still, the US had five of ten most profitable banks in 1992 while Japan had no bank in the top ten in profitability (see Saunders and Walter 1994). In an attempt to create a level financial playing field, the Basle Accord of 1988 set minimum capital requirements for all internationally active banks. Although Japanese bankers and regulators were initially slow to react, the 1990s saw an increase in bad loan write-offs as the Japanese banking industry began restructuring. Since 1997 three internationally active banks, Hokkaido Takushoku, Long-Term Credit Bank and Nippon Credit have been nationalized as a consequence of their bad loan portfolios. The threat of bank insolvency initially gave foreign depositors a 125-basis point premium at Japanese banks in 1997. This premium has subsequently narrowed to ten to twenty basis points (see Mattione 2000).

There has long been debate about whether finance plays an active or passive role in the process of development. Despite the bursting of the asset price bubble and problems at Japanese banks, Japan's real GDP grew from 1990-1996 before experiencing a downturn in 1997. The slow growth rates (termed a growth recession by some) may however, have had their origins in the frailty of the Japanese banking system and by Japanese banks' close lending relationships with commercial borrowers. Recent research has found evidence that monetary policy and other shocks to Japanese banks have been transmitted not only to the domestic economy, but also to the US. (Peek and Rosengren 1997, 2000)

9.3 Method

The technology that banks face is determined not just by the employment of inputs like labor, capital and debt (deposits and other borrowed funds), but also by the ownership structure measured by equity capital. Some bank owners may prefer a 'quiet life' and seek to protect equity capital through greater monitoring of the bank loan and security portfolio by bank employees. Monitoring uses scarce resources and results in lower profits. Other bank owners are willing to bear greater risks if higher profits are forthcoming. In addition, the Basle Accords require internationally active banks to maintain a minimum risk-based capital requirement of 8 percent and banks operating only in domestic markets to maintain a minimum risk-based capital requirement of 4 percent. Ignoring the effects of equity capital would thus bias measures of efficiency and profitability. We follow Hughes and Mester (1998) and Devaney and Weber (2002) and control for bank equity capital in the construction of the technology. Thus, banks of a similar equity structure are compared with one another when measuring profitability and efficiency.

Following Färe and Grosskopf in the previous sections we assume there are $k = 1, ..., K$ banks which employ $x^k \in \Re^N_+$ inputs to produce $y^k \in \Re^M_+$ outputs. The technology for each bank is written as: $\{T^k = \{(x^k, y^k) :$ inputs can produce outputs $\}$. The piecewise linear DEA technology is written as:

$$
\begin{aligned}
T^k = \{(x,y) : \quad & \textstyle\sum_{k=1}^K z_k x_{kn} \leqq x_n, & n = 1, \ldots, N \\
& \textstyle\sum_{k=1}^K z_k y_{km} \geqq y_m, & m = 1, \ldots, M \\
& \textstyle\sum_{k=1}^K z_k = 1, & k = 1, \ldots, K \\
& z_k \geqq 0, & k = 1, \ldots, K\}.
\end{aligned}
\tag{3.86}
$$

The intensity variables,$z_k, k = 1, \ldots, K$, serve to form linear combinations of all observed banks' inputs and outputs. The N+M inequality constraints restrict the technology in that for a particular bank no more output can be produced using no less input than a linear combination of all observed inputs and outputs. Requiring the intensity variables to sum to one allow variable returns to scale so that maximal profits can be positive, negative, or zero. We assume that the first N-1 inputs, such as labor, capital, and deposits are variable inputs (x^v) and can be used in greater or lesser amounts at the bank manager's discretion, but that the Nth input, equity capital (e), is fixed exogenously by bank regulators and owners. Therefore, we partition bank k's input vector as $x^k = (x^{vk}, e^k)$. Define the directional technology distance function for each bank as

$$\vec{D}_T^k(x^{vk}, e^k, y^k; g_x, g_e, g_y) = \sup\{\beta : (x^{vk} - \beta g_x, e^k - \beta g_e, y^k + \beta g_y) \in T^k\} \tag{3.87}$$

where variable inputs are contracted in the direction g_x, equity capital is contracted in the direction g_e , and outputs are expanded in the direction g_y. Throughout the remainder of the paper we choose $g_e = 0$ so that equity capital is not scaled upon. For $(x^{vk}, e^k, y^k) \in T^k$ a value of $\vec{D}_T^k(x^{vk}, e^k, y^k; g_x, 0, g_y) = 0$ indicates that the bank operates on the frontier of T^k and is efficient for the direction $(g_x, 0, g_y)$. Values of $\vec{D}_T^k(x^{vk}, e^k, y^k; g_x, 0, g_y) > 0$ indicate inefficiency. For the DEA technology the directional technology distance function for bank k' is estimated as

$$\begin{aligned} \vec{D}_T^k(x^{vk}, e^k, y^k; g_x, 0, g_y) = & \quad \max \beta \\ & \text{subject to} \\ \sum_{k=1}^{K} z_k x_{kn}^v \leqq x_{k'n}^v - \beta g_x, & \quad n = 1, \ldots, N-1 \\ \sum_{k=1}^{K} z_k e_k \leqq e_{k'}, & \\ \sum_{k=1}^{K} z_k y_{km} \geqq y_{k'm} + \beta g_y, & \quad m = 1, \ldots, M \\ \sum_{k=1}^{K} z_k = 1, & \quad k = 1, \ldots, K \\ z_k \geqq 0, & \quad k = 1, \ldots, K \end{aligned} \tag{3.88}$$

To estimate $\vec{D}_T^k(x^{vk}, e^k, y^k; g_x, 0, g_y)$ as above, the N-1 variable inputs are contracted but the technology is dependent on the amount of equity capital employed.

Given output prices $p \in \Re_+^M$ and variable input prices $w \in \Re_+^{N-1}$ the maximal profit function for bank k' is:

$$\Pi^{k'}(p, w, e^{k'}) = \text{ maximize } \{py - wx^v : (x^v, e^{k'}, y) \in T^{k'}\} \tag{3.89}$$

For the DEA technology the profit function takes the form

$$\begin{aligned}
\Pi^{k'}(p, w, e^{k'}) = \quad & \text{maximize } (py - wx^v) && (3.90)\\
\text{subject to} & \\
\sum_{k=1}^{K} z_k x_{kn}^v \leqq x_n^v, \quad & n = 1, \ldots, N-1\\
\sum_{k=1}^{K} z_k e_k \leqq e_{k'}, & \\
\sum_{k=1}^{K} z_k y_{km} \geqq y_m, \quad & m = 1, \ldots, M\\
\sum_{k=1}^{K} z_k = 1, \quad & k = 1, \ldots, K\\
z_k \geqq 0, \quad & k = 1, \ldots, K.
\end{aligned}$$

In (3.88) the outputs, $y_{km}, m = 1, ..., M$, and inputs, $x_{kn}, n = 1, ..., N$, of bank k' enter on the right-hand side of the constraints defining the technology, while in (3.89) the bank chooses outputs, $y_m, m = 1, ..., M$, and variable inputs, $x_n^v, n = 1, ..., N-1$, to maximize profits given the technology which depends on the amount of equity capital, $e_{k'}$ employed.

We know that $(x^{vk}, e^k, y^k) \in T^k$ if and only if

$$(x^{vk} - \vec{D}_T^k(x^{vk}, e^k, y^k; g_x, 0, g_y)g_x, e^k, y^k + \vec{D}_T^k(x^{vk}, e^k, y^k; g_x, 0, g_y)g_y) \in T^k. \quad (3.91)$$

Therefore,

$$\begin{aligned}
\Pi(p, w, e^k) \quad \geqq \quad & (py - wx^{vk}) + p\vec{D}_T^k(x^{vk}, e^k, y^k; g_x, 0, g_y)g_y \quad (3.92)\\
& + w\vec{D}_T^k(x^{vk}, e^k, y^k; g_x, 0, g_y)g_x.
\end{aligned}$$

In words, maximal profit is no less than actual profits plus the gain in profit that could be realized by a reduction in technical inefficiency. The reduction in technical inefficiency is composed of two parts: the gain in revenue from an expansion in outputs to the frontier, given as $p\vec{D}_T^k(x^{vk}, e^k, y^k; g_x, 0, g_y)g_y$ and the reduction in costs from the use of fewer inputs, $w\vec{D}_T^k(x^{vk}, e^k, y^k; g_x, 0, g_y)g_x$. The inequality arises because even if all technical inefficiency is eliminated the bank might still not choose to allocate resources efficiently. Subtracting actual profits from both sides of (3.92), normalizing by $(pg_y + wg_x)$, and then adding an allocative efficiency component ($\vec{AE}_{T^k}$) yields the measure of Nerlovian profit efficiency:

$$\frac{\Pi(p,w,e^k) - (py - wx^{vk})}{pg_y + wg_x} = \vec{D}_T^k(x^{vk}, e^k, y^k; g_x, 0, g_y) + \vec{AE}_{T^k}, \tag{3.93}$$

where the left-hand side of (3.93) is Nerlovian profit efficiency for bank k and the right-hand side is the sum of bank k's technical efficiency and allocative efficiency. Values of Nerlovian profit efficiency, technical efficiency, or allocative efficiency equal to zero indicate the bank is overall profit efficient, technically efficient, or allocatively efficient. Values of any of the efficiency indicators greater than zero denote inefficiency. As Koopmans (1957) has shown, the industry technology set, T, may be defined as the sum of each individual firm's technology set, $T = \sum_{k=1}^K T^k$. Let industry variable inputs equal $x^v = \sum_{k=1}^K x^{vk}$ and let industry outputs equal $y = \sum_{k=1}^K y^k$. The maximal industry profit function for industry technology T is

$$\begin{aligned} \Pi(p,w,e^1,\ldots,e^K) &= \max\{py - wx^v : \\ &\quad (\sum_{k=1}^K x^{vk}, e^1, \ldots, e^K, \sum_{k=1}^K y^k) \in T\} \\ &= \sum_{k=1}^K \Pi^k(p,w,e^k). \end{aligned} \tag{3.94}$$

The directional technology distance function defined on T for the industry is $\vec{D}_T(\sum_{k=1}^K x^{vk}, e^1, \ldots, e^K, \sum_{k=1}^K y^k; g_x, 0, g_y)$. The Nerlovian profit efficiency indicator (NI) for the industry can be decomposed into indicators of industry technical efficiency and industry allocative efficiency:

$$\frac{\Pi(p,w,e^1,\ldots,e^K) - (p\sum_{k=1}^K y^k - w\sum_{k=1}^K x^{vk})}{pg_y + wg_x} = \vec{D}_T(\sum_{k=1}^K x^{vk}, e^1, \ldots, e^K, \sum_{k=1}^K y^k; g_x, 0, g_y) + \vec{AE}_T. \tag{3.95}$$

We note that the industry Nerlovian profit indicator depends on the distribution of equity capital between the K banks and not just on the aggregate level of equity capital. When does industry technical efficiency equal the sum of the technical efficiencies of the individual banks? By summing over the K banks, industry technical efficiency equals the sum of each bank's technical efficiency when $\vec{AE}_T = \sum_{k=1}^{K} \vec{AE}_{T^k}$. A special case of this condition occurs when each bank has allocated resources efficiently; $\vec{AE}_{T^k} = 0, k = 1, \ldots, K$.

Over time changes in prices, changes in technical or allocative efficiency, or technical change may cause banks to become more or less profitable. Again following Färe and Grosskopf suppose that production takes place during t=1,...,T periods. The Luenberger profitability change indicator for bank k takes the form:

$$\mathrm{L}(x^{vk,t}, e^{k,t}, y^{k,t}, x^{vk,t+1}, e^{k,t+1}, y^{k,t+1}) = \tag{3.96}$$

$$\begin{aligned} 1/2[&(\Pi^{k,t+1}(p^t, w^t, e^{k,t}) - \Pi^{k,t+1}(p^{t+1}, w^{t+1}, e^{k,t+1}))/(p^{t+1}g_y + w^{t+1}g_x) \\ &+(\Pi^{k,t}(p^t, w^t, e^{k,t}) - \Pi^{k,t}(p^{t+1}, w^{t+1}, e^{k,t+1}))/(p^{t+1}g_y + w^{t+1}g_x)] \end{aligned}$$

If the bank has allocated resources efficiently, then $\vec{AE}_{T^k} = 0$, and

$$\frac{\Pi^{k,t+1}(p^t, w^t, e^{k,t})}{p^t g_y + w^t g_x} = \vec{D}_T^{k,t+1}(x^{vk,t}, e^{k,t}, y^{k,t}; g_x, 0, g_y), \tag{3.97}$$

and

$$\frac{\Pi^{k,t}(p^t, w^t, e^{k,t})}{p^t g_y + w^t g_x} = \vec{D}_T^{k,t}(x^{vk,t}, e^{k,t}, y^{k,t}; g_x, 0, g_y), \tag{3.98}$$

and

$$\frac{\Pi^{k,t}(p^{t+1}, w^{t+1}, e^{k,t+1})}{p^{t+1} g_y + w^{t+1} g_x} = \vec{D}_T^{k,t}(x^{vk,t+1}, e^{k,t+1}, y^{k,t+1}; g_x, 0, g_y). \tag{3.99}$$

Efficient resource allocation therefore allows (3.96) to serve as a primal productivity indicator for bank K. For the industry, a Luenberger profitability change indicator (or a primal productivity indicator) can be estimated as the sum of the bank's Luenberger profit indicators or technical efficiency indicators:

$$\mathrm{L}(\sum_{k=1}^{K} x^{vk,t}, e^{1,t}, \ldots, e^{K,t}, \sum_{k=1}^{K} y^{k,t}, \sum_{k=1}^{K} x^{vk,t+1}, e^{1,t+1}, \ldots, e^{K,t+1}, \sum_{k=1}^{K} y^{k,t+1})$$
$$= \sum_{k=1}^{K} \mathrm{L}(x^{vk,t}, e^{k,t}, y^{k,t}, x^{vk,t+1}, e^{k,t+1}, y^{k,t+1}).$$

Values of the Luenberger profit indicator greater than zero indicate increases in profitability or productivity; values less than zero indicate declines in profitability or productivity from period t to period t+1.

9.4 Data and Results

We employ data on Japanese banks operating during 1992-1996 to estimate industry efficiency and profitability (productivity) change. Given an equity capital structure (e) banks transform variable inputs of labor (x1), physical capital (x2), and funds from customers (x3), to produce loans (y1) and security investments and other interest bearing assets (y2). This specification is consistent with the asset approach of Sealey and Lindley (1977). Fukuyama and Weber (2002) provide a complete description of the data and the specification of bank outputs and inputs. Table 1 presents descriptive statistics for the pooled data. The number of banks ranged from 141 in 1992, to 140 in 1993-1995, to 136 in 1996.

To implement the Nerlovian profit efficiency indicator given by (3.93) we assume that all banks in a given year face the mean output-input price vector for that year. For example, in 1992 p=(0.0590, 0.0441) and w=(0.0077, 0.4712, 0.0368). Table 2 presents the means and standard deviations for actual profit and maximal profit as well as the optimal outputs (y*) and optimal inputs (x*) found as the solution to (3.90). We also need to choose a directional vector, $g = (g_x, 0, g_y)$, common to all banks to aggregate the measures technical efficiency. If each bank's technology is such that the maximal profit function yields optimal outputs and optimal inputs which are the same for all banks, then a natural direction yielding for k=1,...,K banks is $g = (x^{v*}, 0, y^*)$. Unfortunately, the optimal outputs and optimal inputs varied for each bank (note the positive standard deviations for $y*$ and x^{v*}). Therefore, we measure technical efficiency in the direction $g = (1, 0, 1)$ for every year.[3] This directional vector implies that the directional technology distance function gives an estimate of the maximum unit expansion in outputs and

[3] One could also take $g = (\overline{x}^v, 0, \overline{y})$ where the bars refer to the mean value of the vectors for the firms in the sample. In this case $(pg_y + wg_x) = p\overline{y} + w\overline{x}^v$.

the unit contraction in inputs. It also implies that the denominator of the Nerlovian profit efficiency indicator, $(pg_y + wg_x)$, equals the sum of the output and input prices faced by each firm. For 1992, $(pg_y + wg_x)$ = (.0590 x 1 + .0441 x 1 + .0077 x 1 + .4712 x 1 + .0368 x 1) = .6188. The decomposition of the Nerlovian profit efficiency indicator is reported in Table 2 for each of the years. Recall that values of the indicators equal to zero signify efficiency and values of the indicators greater than zero signify inefficiency. In 1992 the arithmetic mean value of $\vec{D}_T^{k,t}(x^{vk,t}, e^{k,t}, y^{k,t}; 1, 0, 1)$ is 0.0081 indicating that on average, banks could expand both loans and other investments by 0.0081 trillion (8.1 billion) yen and contract labor by 8.1=0.0081 x 1000 full-time employees and contract physical capital and funds by 8.1 billion yen given the technology. Technical inefficiency increased from 1992-1994 and then declined throughout the remainder of the period.

The Nerlovian profit efficiency indicator equals the difference between maximal and actual profits (normalized). In 1992 mean maximal profits are 0.063 trillion yen and mean actual profits are 0.0451 trillion yen. Given the normalization, =0.6188, the mean Nerlovian profit efficiency indicator is 0.029=(0.0630 - 0.0451)/0.6188.[4] Nerlovian profit efficiency declines during 1992-93 indicating greater profit efficiency, increases during 1994 and 1995 indicating less profit efficiency, and then declines in 1996 but remains at a higher level than in 1992. The residual difference between Nerlovian profit efficiency and technical efficiency is allocative efficiency and it follows the same pattern as Nerlovian profit efficiency throughout the period.

We earlier posed the question: When is the industry technical efficiency indicator equal to the sum of the banks' technical efficiency indicators? Since maximal industry profit equals the sum of the banks' maximal profits, the answer is if the industry allocative efficiency indicator equals the sum of the bank's allocative efficiency indicators. A special case of this condition occurs when each bank's allocative efficiency equals zero. To test this special case we use an Anova F-test and a battery of non-parametric tests to test the hypothesis that the bank Nerlovian profit efficiency indicator (NI) equals the bank's directional technology distance function. If the Nerlovian profit efficiency indicator has the same ranking as the directional technology distance function then there is some evidence that a bank's resources are allocated effi-

[4]In 1993 $(pg_y + wg_x) = 0.5938$. In 1994 $(pg_y + wg_x) = 0.5874$. In 1995 $(pg_y + wg_x) = 0.5781$, and in 1996 $(pg_y + wg_x) = 0.6108$.

ciently. Table 3 presents the results of these tests for each of the years. The tests strongly reject the null hypothesis for all years indicating that resources are not allocated efficiently at the bank level.[5]

Finally, we aggregate the individual bank Nerlovian profit efficiency indicators and the Luenberger profitability change indicators to the industry level. We subdivide the banking industry into city banks and regional banks. City banks are large in size, have branches throughout the country, help finance large business and yield nationwide influence. Regional banks focus more on local business with small and medium-sized companies their primary customers. City banks number eleven in 1992 and decline to ten in 1996. Regional banks number 130 in 1992 and decline to 126 in 1996. Figure 1 illustrates industry Nerlovian profit efficiency for city banks, regional banks and the industry. Total industry inefficiency (NI) increases from 1992 to 1995 and then falls in 1996. While city banks became more profit inefficient throughout the period, they accounted for between only 8.8% and 12.2% of industry profit inefficiency. Figure 2 shows the industry Luenberger profitability change indicator (L). Industry profitability grows from 1992 to 1993 and is positive for both city and regular banks. During 1993-1994 though, industry profitability declines sharply with city banks leading the way. However, by 1994-95 industry profitability rebounds and is positive for both city and regional banks before falling during 1995-96 to about zero with gains by regional banks just a little more than offset by losses by city banks. Our results compare well with those of Maudos and Pastor (2001). They estimate profit efficiency for a sample of sixteen countries, including fourteen from the European Union, Japan, and the US. Specifying industry profit efficiency as the ratio of actual to maximal industry profit and estimating it using a stochastic frontier approach, they find profit efficiency in Japan declining from 1992 to 1994 before rising in 1995.

9.5 Summary

Many studies have examined the efficiency and productivity growth of financial institutions. If industry efficiency and productivity change are the primary focus of policy makers and regulators then it is important to be able to consistently aggregate from the financial institution to the financial industry. In this paper we estimate the Nerlovian profit

[5]We also test whether the Nerlovian profit efficiency indicator is equal to the allocative efficiency indicator for each of the years. We reject the null hypothesis of equality for 1992 to 1995 at the 5% signficance level but are unable to reject the null for 1996.

efficiency indicator for Japanese banks and consistently aggregate the profit efficiency indicator for each bank to the industry level. Our results indicate that the Japanese banking industry is less profit efficient in 1996 than 1992. While our focus in this paper is on the Japanese banking industry, an interesting extension of the method would be to examine a wider variety of financial institutions. In Japan (as in other countries) banks, credit cooperatives, insurance companies, and securities firms are all similar in that they transform labor, physical capital, and a source of funds into various kinds of loans and investments. Recent research has examined the efficiency of each of these Japanese financial institutions separately. Aggregating to a Japanese financial institutions' industry would be a natural extension of the method described in this paper.

Table 1
Descriptive Statistics for Japanese Banks, 1992-1996

Variable	*Mean*	*St.Dev.*	*Min.*	*Max.*
y1=loans	3.295	7.213	0.097	43.75
y2=oth. inv.	1.364	3.161	0.036	26.629
$p1^c$	0.043	0.011	0.005	0.071
$p2^c$	0.040	0.011	0.004	0.117
x1=labor[b]	2.831	3.603	0.329	22.350
x2=capital[a]	0.041	0.070	0.002	0.423
x3=funds[a]	4.518	10.030	0.132	68.324
w1[d]	0.008	0.001	0.001	0.013
w2[c]	0.483	0.120	0.057	1.125
w3[c]	0.023	0.010	0.002	0.068
e=equity[a]	0.182	0.389	0.004	2.794
py-wx^v=obs. prof.	0.049	0.142	-0.004	1.119
$\Pi(p, w, e)$ =max. prof.	0.073	0.147	-0.001	1.119

Notes
a: trillions of yen
b: 1000s FTE empl.
c: yen per yen
d: billions of yen

Table 2
Decomposition of Bank Profit Inefficiency
Means (standard deviations)

Variable	1992	1993	1994	1995	1996
# of banks	141	140	140	140	136
$py - wx_v$	0.0451	0.0409	0.0517	0.0522	0.0546
(obs. prof.)	(0.1310)	(0.1204)	(0.1430)	(0.1471)	(0.1672)
$\pi(p, w, e)$	0.0630	0.0579	0.0726	0.0907	0.0843
(max. prof.)	(0.1350)	(0.1226)	(0.1474)	(0.1495)	(0.1733)
y_1*	3.7579	3.5327	3.5686	5.8594	4.4350
	(7.4640)	(7.3447)	(7.1319)	(7.1023)	(8.0144)
y_2*	1.4028	1.6622	1.6627	1.9423	1.8042
	(2.9033)	(3.1245)	(3.1130)	(2.9144)	(3.4789)
x_1*	2.3348	2.4715	2.3867	4.3303	2.8878
	(3.7471)	(4.1381)	(3.7794)	(3.1863)	(3.6246)
x_2*	0.0358	0.0314	0.0311	0.0642	0.0407
	(0.0697)	(0.0670)	(0.0648)	(0.0540)	(0.0095)
x_3*	5.0469	5.0851	5.0766	7.5568	6.0396
	(10.1116)	(10.2224)	(9.9635)	(9.6951)	(11.1194)
For $g = (g_x, 0, g_y) = (1, 0, 1)$					
Π effic	0.0290	0.0285	0.0357	0.0666	0.0486
	(0.0287)	(0.0266)	(0.0316)	(0.0369)	(0.0502)
$\vec{D}_T(x^v, e, y; g)$	0.0081	0.0081	0.0084	0.0082	0.0067
	(0.0121)	(0.0118)	(0.0116)	(0.0096)	(0.0080)
$\vec{AE}_T$	0.0209	0.0204	0.0273	0.0584	0.0419
	(0.0219)	(0.0194)	(0.0255)	(0.0321)	(0.0478)

Table 3
Nonparametric Tests

Is Π Effic $= \vec{D}_T(x^v, e, y; 1, 0, 1)$?

Test	1992	1993	1994	1995	1996
Anova-F	44.19	69.12	91.98	328.40	92.44
$(prob > F)$	(0.01)	(0.01)	(0.01)	(0.01)	(0.01)
Wilcoxon-χ^2	65.34	76.68	99.44	166.68	109.39
$(prob > \chi^2)$	(0.01)	(0.01)	(0.01)	(0.01)	(0.01)
Median-χ^2	37.02	47.89	82.22	166.03	75.96
$(prob > \chi^2)$	(0.01)	(0.01)	(0.01)	(0.01)	(0.01)
Savage-χ^2	49.34	62.18	77.41	118.82	87.80
$(prob > \chi^2)$	(0.01)	(0.01)	(0.01)	(0.01)	(0.01)
Van der Waerden-χ^2	63.82	73.38	92.57	145.51	103.47
$(prob > \chi^2)$	(0.01)	(0.01)	(0.01)	(0.01)	(0.01)
Kolmogorov-Smirnov	3.57	4.06	4.72	6.63	4.91
$(prob > KSa)$	(0.01)	(0.01)	(0.01)	(0.01)	(0.01)

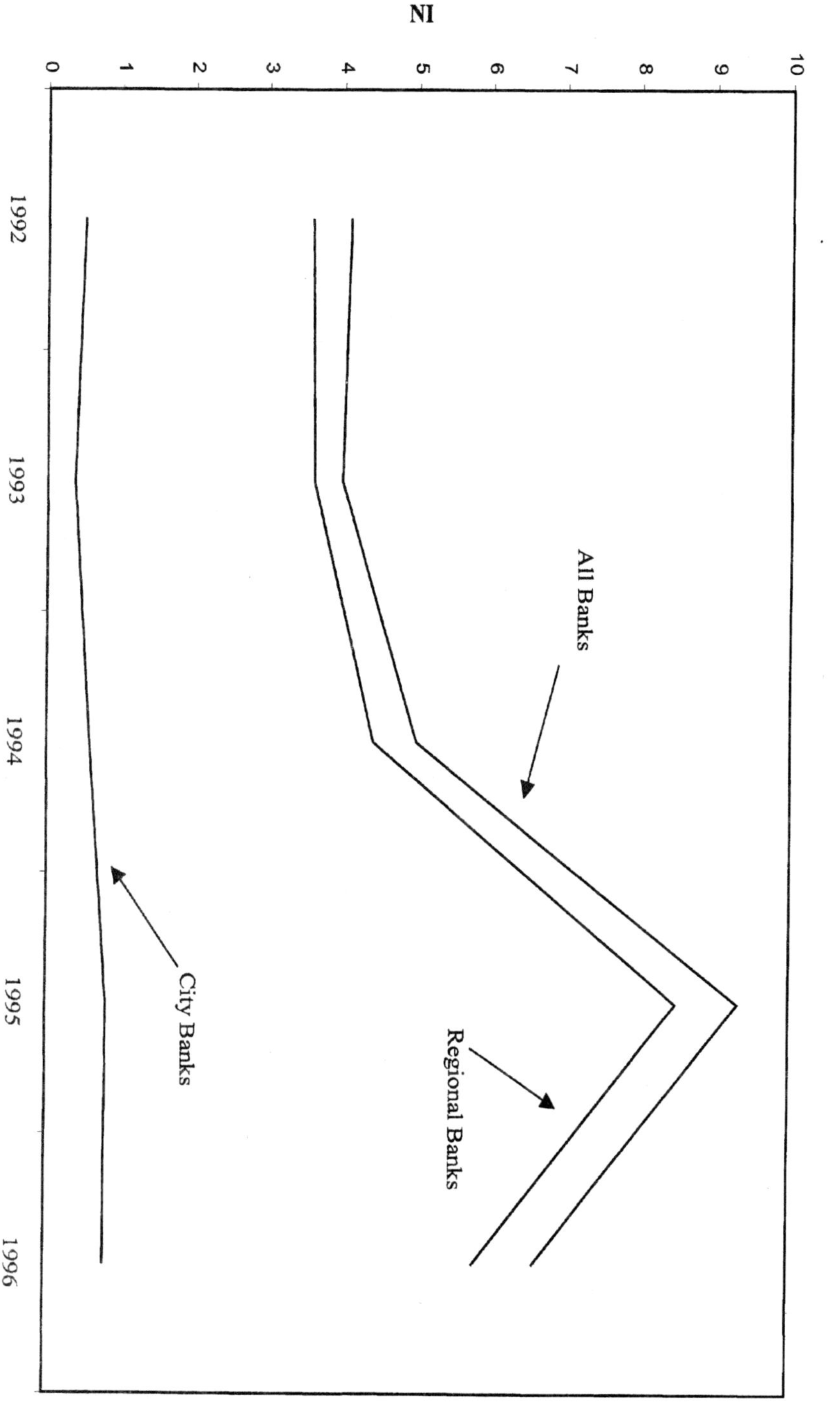

Figure 3.5. The Industry Nerlovian Profit Efficiency Indicator (NI)

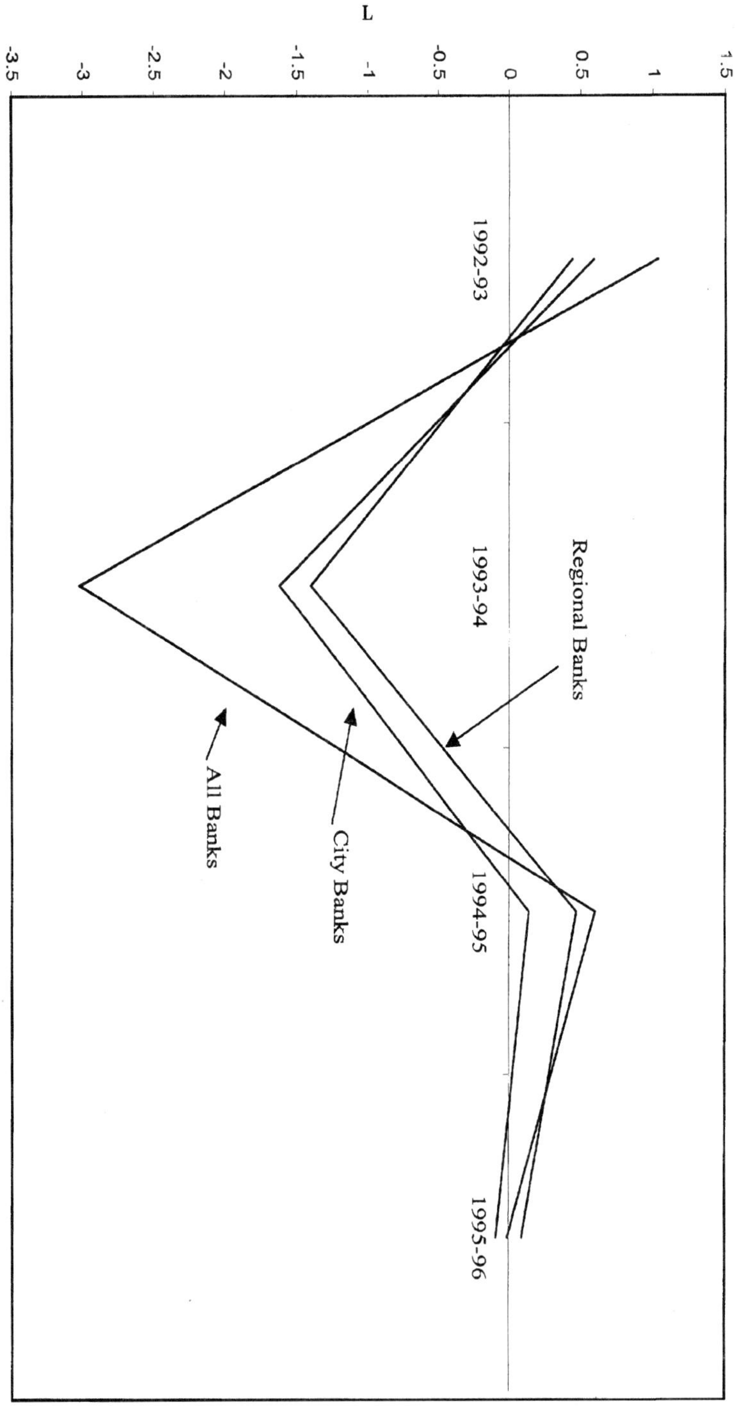

Figure 3.6. The Industry Luenberger Profitability Change Indicator (L)

10. Remarks on the Literature

The Fox Paradox was introduced by Fox (1999) and studied by Färe and Grosskopf (2000). Here we use it to show that there is a close connection between aggregation and the functional form of the efficiency models being aggregated.

Koopmans' Theorem appears in various microeconomics textbooks such as Varian (1992), Mas-Colell et al. (1995) and Luenberger (1995). The Luenberger reference includes a geometric interpretation of the theorem.

The sections covering aggregation across firms for both indicators and indexes are extensions of Färe, Grosskopf and Zelenyuk (2001) and Färe and Zelenyuk (2002). A survey of the indexes is found in Ylvinger (2000).

Aggregation across inputs and outputs in the activity analysis or DEA efficiency framework has been considered by Färe and Grosskopf (1985) and Färe and Zelenyuk (2002).

Färe and Primont (2002) extend the analysis of the Luenberger aggregation to the consideration of approximation methods. Balk (1998) also discusses the Luenberger productivity indicator and its dual indicator, the profit function approach.

The section on aggregation and decomposition is based on Färe and Zelenyuk (2002).

11. Appendix: Proofs

Proof of Profit Theorem from Mas-Colell et al. (1995), p. 148.

Let $(x^k, y^k) \in T^k, k = 1, \ldots, K$. Then $(\sum_{k=1}^K x^k, \sum_{k=1}^K y^k) \in T$ and by profit maximization $\Pi(p, w) \geqq p\sum_{k=1}^K y^k - w\sum_{k=1}^K x^k = \sum_{k=1}^K (py^k - wx^k)$.
Thus $\Pi(p, w) \geqq \sum_{k=1}^K \Pi^k(p, w)$.

Next let $(x, y) \in T$, then there exists $(x^k, y^k) \in T^k$ such that $x = \sum_{k=1}^K x^k, y = \sum_{k=1}^K y^k$ by the definition of T. Now $py - wx = \sum_{k=1}^K (py^k - wx^k) \leqq \sum_{k=1}^K \Pi^k(p, w)$.

Since $(x, y) \in T$ is arbitrary,
$\Pi(p, w) \leqq \sum_{k=1}^K \Pi^k(p, w)$, and the two inequalities

$\Pi(p,w) \leqq \sum_{k=1}^{K} \Pi^k(p,w) \leqq \Pi(p,w)$ yield the result.
Q.E.D.

Proof of Revenue Corollary.

Let $y^k \in P^k(x^k)$ then $\sum_{k=1}^{K} y^k \in P(x^1,\ldots,x^K)$ and hence $R(x^1,\ldots,x^K,p) \geqq p\sum_{k=1}^{K} y^k = \sum_{k=1}^{K} py^k$. Thus $R(x^1,\ldots,x^K,p) \geqq \sum_{k=1}^{K} R^k(x^k,p)$.
Conversely assume that $y \in P(x^1,\ldots,x^K)$, then by the definition of $P(x^1,\ldots,x^K)$ there are $y^k \in P^k(x^k)$ such that $y = \sum_{k=1}^{K} y^k$. Now $py = \sum py^k \leqq \sum_{k=1}^{K} R^k(x^k,p)$.
Finally,
$R(x^1,\ldots,x^K,p) \leqq \sum_{k=1}^{K} R^k(x^k,p)$,
and the corollary follows from
$R(x^1,\ldots,x^K,p) \leqq \sum_{k=1}^{K} R^k(x^k,p) \leqq R(x^1,\ldots,x^K,p)$.
Q.E.D.

Proof of Cost Corollary.
This is left for the reader.

Proof of

$$SCI(y^{k'},c_{k'\hat{N}},x_{k'\hat{N}+1},\ldots,x_{k'N};g_{x_{\hat{N}}}) = \vec{AD}_i(y^{k'},c_{k'\hat{N}},x_{k'\hat{N}+1},\ldots,x_{k'N};g_{x_{\hat{N}}}).$$

Consider the problem

$$\begin{aligned} &\max \beta \\ &s.t. \quad \sum_{k=1}^{K} z_k y_{km} \geqq y_{k'm}, && m = 1,\ldots,M, \\ &\sum_{k=1}^{K} z_k x_{kn} \leqq x_{k'n} - \beta g_{x_n}, && n = 1,\ldots,\hat{N}, \\ &\sum_{k=1}^{K} z_k x_{kn} \leqq x_{k'n}, && n = \hat{N}+1,\ldots,N, \\ &z_k \geqq 0, && k = 1,\ldots,K. \end{aligned}$$

Multiply the $n = 1,\ldots,\hat{N}$ constraints by w_n and add them together, then we have

$$\sum_{k=1}^{K} z_k \sum_{n=1}^{\hat{N}} c_{kn} \leqq c_{k'\hat{N}} - \beta \sum_{n=1}^{\hat{N}} w_n g_{x_n}.$$

Thus the problem may be written as

$$\begin{aligned} \max \quad & \frac{c_{k'\hat{N}} - \sum_{k=1}^{K} c_{k\hat{n}}}{\sum_{n=1}^{\hat{N}} w_n g_{xn}} \\ s.t. \quad & \textstyle\sum_{k=1}^{K} z_k y_{km} \geqq y_{k'm}, \quad m = 1, \ldots, M, \\ & \textstyle\sum_{k=1}^{K} z_k x_{kn} \leqq x_{k'n}, \quad n = \hat{N}+1, \ldots, N, \\ & z_k \geqq 0, \quad k = 1, \ldots, K. \end{aligned}$$

From the cost minimization problem in the text it follows that

$$C(y^{k'}, w_1, \ldots, w_{\hat{N}}, x_{k'\hat{N}+1}, \ldots, x_{k'N}) = \sum_{n=1}^{\hat{N}} z_k c_{kn},$$

proving our claim.
Q.E.D.

Proof of

$$C(y^{k'}, w_1, \ldots, w_{\hat{N}}, x_{k'\hat{N}+1}, \ldots, x_{k'N}) = AF_i(y^{k'}, c_{k'\hat{N}}, x_{k'\hat{N}+1}, \ldots, x_{k'N}.$$

Use the previous proof and set $g_{x_n} = x_{k'n}, n = 1, \ldots, \hat{N}$.
Q.E.D.

Chapter 4

APPENDIX: AXIOMS OF PRODUCTION

The intention of this appendix is to make our book self-contained. Since most readers of these essays will have some familiarity with axiomatic production theory, this appendix is meant to serve as a reference or reminder of the relevant concepts. Consequently, we give only a rudimentary description of the basic axioms of production; for a more complete discussion see Färe and Grosskopf (1996), Färe and Primont (1995) or Shephard (1970).

We begin with the static production technology which transforms **Input Vectors**

$$x = (x_1, \ldots, x_N) \in \Re_+^N$$

into **Output Vectors**

$$y = (y_1, \ldots, y_M) \in \Re_+^M$$

and which can be represented in three equivalent ways: 1) by its graph, 2) by its output correspondence or 3) by its input correspondence.

The graph of **Technology** consists of all feasible input-output vectors, i.e.,

$$T = \{(x, y) : x \text{ can produce } y\}.$$

Thus if $(x, y) \in T$ then and only then can the input vector x produce the output vector y. For the single input-output case, the boundary of the technology is also known as the total product curve.

The **Output Correspondence** is the second representation of the technology—it is defined in terms of the graph as

$$P : \Re_+^N \to P(x) = \{y : (x, y) \in T\}. \tag{4.1}$$

The images of this correspondence are the **Output Sets** $P(x)$, which consist of all output vectors that can be produced by a given input vector $x \in \Re_+^N$. The definition above shows how these sets–also known as production possibility sets–and the output correspondence are defined in terms of the graph of technology, T.

Next we show that T can be retrieved from the output sets, thus proving that T and the output sets–or equivalently the output correspondence–provide the same information about the technology. Specifically, we can define T as

$$T = \{(x, y) : y \in P(x), x \in \Re_+^N\}.$$

The third representation of the technology is the **Input Correspondence** which may also be defined in terms of the graph

$$L : \Re_+^M \to L(y) = \{x : (x, y) \in T\}. \tag{4.2}$$

The images of the input correspondence $L(y), y \in \Re_+^M$ are called the **Input Requirement Sets** or **Input Sets** for short. An input set $L(y)$ consists of all input vectors that can produce the output vector y. The technology T can also be retrieved from the input sets, specifically

$$T = \{(x, y) : x \in L(y), y \in \Re_+^M\}. \tag{4.3}$$

The results above demonstrate the following proposition

Proposition A.1: $y \in P(x) \Leftrightarrow (x, y) \in T \Leftrightarrow x \in L(y)$,

which tells us that the output and input sets are equivalent representations of technology, as is T.

Proposition (A.1) is illustrated in Figure 4.1. The technology T consists of the input-output combinations (x, y) that are on and between the broken line and the x-axis. The input set associated with the output level y^o is $L(y^o)$ where $L(y^o) = [x^o, +\infty)$. The output set associated with input x^o is $P(x^o)$ where $P(x^o) = [0, y^o]$.

Under the axiomatic approach to production theory—which we follow here—the technology or production model is assumed to satisfy certain

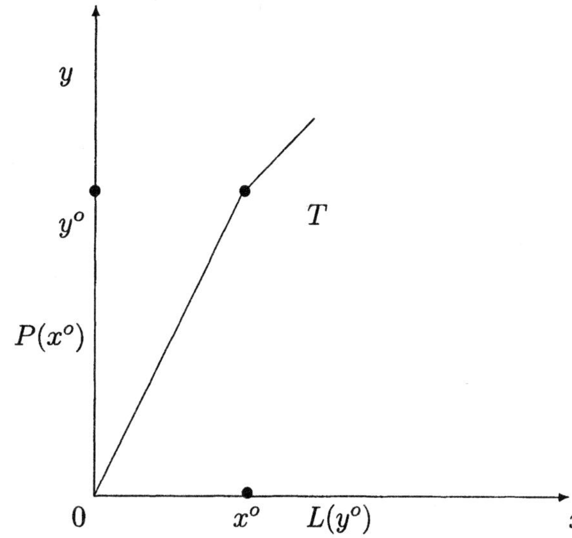

Figure 4.1. Illustration of Proposition A.1

properties or axioms. Due to Proposition (A.1) these properties can equivalently be stated on T, the output sets $P(x), x \in \Re_+^N$ or on the input sets $L(y), y \in \Re_+^M$. Below we choose the representation of technology that best illustrates the particular axiom.

Axioms:

A.1(a) $0 \in P(x), \forall x \in \Re_+^N$,

A.1(b) $y \notin P(0), y \geqq 0, y \neq 0$.

The first part (a) of axiom **A.1** states that inactivity is always possible, that is, zero output can be produced by any input vector $x \in \Re_+^N$. Part (b) states that it is impossible to produce output without any inputs, i.e., there is no free lunch. Together (a) and (b) imply that $P(0) = \{0\}$, i.e., only zero output is feasible when there is no input used $(x = 0)$.

Input disposability is modeled by two axioms:

A.2 $x \in L(y)$ and $\lambda \geqq 1 \Rightarrow \lambda x \in L(y)$.

A.2.S $x \geqq x^o \in L(y) \Rightarrow x \in L(y)$.

Weak Disposability of Inputs is modeled by **A.2** and it says that if all inputs are increased proportionally by λ, then output will not decrease, i.e, if $x \in L(y)$, then $\lambda x \in L(y)$, for $\lambda \geqq 1$. On the other hand, if inputs are not increased proportionally, output may decrease. To see this suppose that the technology is modeled by the following production function,

$$\begin{aligned} y &= (x_1 - x_2)^{1/2} x_2^{1/2}, \text{ if } x_1 \geqq x_2, \\ y &= 0, \text{ if } x_1 < x_2. \end{aligned}$$

Now if the input vector (x_1, x_2) is increased proportionally by λ, then output—if positive—is also increased by λ, i.e, the function is homogeneous of degree + 1 and hence satisfies **A.2**. On the other hand if x_1 is positive and given, say $x_1 = \hat{x}_1$, then as x_2 grows from $x_2 = 0$ to $x_2 = \hat{x}_1$, output first increases and then eventually decreases to zero. In particular when x_2 becomes larger than x_1 output decreases and the marginal product of x_2, $\partial y / \partial x_2$ becomes negative. This is, of course, due to congestion, so **A.2** allows us to model congestion and overutilization of inputs.

Strong Disposability of Inputs, modeled by **A.2.S**, on the other hand precludes congestion. It says that output does not decrease if any or all feasible inputs are increased. Note that if strong disposability applies, so does weak disposability, i.e, **A.2.S** $\Rightarrow$ **A.2** but the converse does not hold.

The input set from our example above, $L(y) = \{(x_1, x_2) : (x_1 - x_2)^{1/2} {x_2}^{1/2} \geqq y\}$ has two asymptotes, one toward the x_1-axis and the other toward the ray described by $x_1 = x_2$, i.e., the isoquant is 'backward-bending'. Now if strong disposability is imposed, the corresponding isoquant would be extended northward instead.

Like inputs, outputs can be weakly or strongly disposable, which we model with the following two axioms.

A.3 $y \in P(x), 0 \leqq \theta \leqq 1 \Rightarrow \theta y \in P(x)$.

A.3.S $y \leqq y^o, y^o \in P(x) \Rightarrow y \in P(x)$.

Axiom **A.3** imposes **Weak Disposability of Outputs**, whereas **A.3.S** imposes **Strong Disposability of Outputs**. These are the output analogs of our input disposability assumptions and prove to be particularly useful in modeling production in the presence of undesirable outputs which is discussed in detail in Essay 2. Here we note that weak disposability allows for *radial* contractions of observed output bundles in a given output set, i.e., reductions of all outputs by the same proportion are always feasible given that available inputs are held constant. Axiom **A.3.S** allows for reductions in outputs given inputs, but those reductions are not required to be proportional for all outputs. Rather, any reductions in one or more outputs, holding inputs and other outputs constant are feasible.

Next we turn to some more technical axioms.

A.4 $\forall x \in \Re_+^N, P(x)$ is **bounded.**

The assumption that $P(x)$ is bounded for each input vector means that only finite amounts of output can be produced from finite amounts of inputs.

A.5 The graph of technology T is a **closed set**,

i.e, if $(x^l, y^l) \to (x^o, y^o)$ and $(x^l, y^l) \in T$ for all l, then $(x^o, y^o) \in T$.

If T is closed, then it follows that both the output sets $P(x), x \in \Re_+^N$ and the input sets $L(y), y \in \Re_+^M$ are also closed sets. Thus the two axioms **A.4** and **A.5** imply that the output sets are compact sets, i.e., closed and bounded in $\Re_+^M$.

Convexity of the input set, the output set and the graph are imposed in order that duality between quantities and prices may apply. We say that the **Input Set is Convex** if

A.6 $\forall y \in \Re_+^M$ if x and $x^o \in L(y)$ and $0 \leqq \lambda \leqq 1$, then $(\lambda x + (1-\lambda)x^o) \in L(y)$.

and that the **Output Set is Convex** if

A.7 $\forall x \in \Re_+^N$, if y and $y^o \in P(x)$ and $0 \leqq \theta \leqq 1$, then $(\theta y + (1-\theta)y^o) \in P(x)$.

It is important to notice that these two convexity assumptions are independent of each other, i.e., **A.6** does not imply **A.7**, nor is the converse true. On the other hand, if T is convex then the input and output sets are also convex. T **is convex** if

A.8 (x, y) and $(x^o, y^o) \in T$ and $0 \leqq \mu \leqq 1$, then $(\mu(x, y)+(1-\mu)(x^o, y^o)) \in T$.

As pointed out above **A.8** implies **A.6** and **A.7**, but **A.6** and/or **A.7** do not imply **A.8**.

Properties concerning returns to scale are taken up next. Constant and nonincreasing returns to scale are readily expressed in terms of T. The technology exhibits **Constant Returns to Scale** (CRS) if

A.9 $\lambda T = T, \lambda > 0,$

i.e., T is a cone. Note that **A.9** is equivalent to

A.9' $P(\lambda x) = \lambda P(x), \lambda > 0,$

and

A.9" $L(\theta y) = \theta L(y), \theta > 0.$

We show that **A.9** holds if and only if **A.9'** holds.

Assume **A.9** is true, then by Proposition A.1

$$\begin{aligned} P(\lambda x) &= \{y : (\lambda x, y) \in T\} \\ &= \lambda\{y/\lambda : (x, y/\lambda) \in (1/\lambda)T\} \\ &= \lambda\{\hat{y} : (x, \hat{y}) \in T\}(\text{use } \mathbf{A.9}) \\ &= \lambda P(x) \end{aligned}$$

To prove that **A.9'** $\Rightarrow$ **A.9** recall that

$$\begin{array}{ccc} y \in P(x) \text{ for all } x \in \Re^N_+ & \Leftrightarrow & \lambda y \in P(\lambda x) \text{ for all } \lambda x \in \Re^N_+ \\ \Updownarrow & & \Updownarrow \\ (x, y) \in T & & (\lambda x, \lambda y) \in T \end{array}$$

Under (global) constant returns to scale the technology is a cone. This is equivalent to the output and input sets satisfying homogeneity of degree

+1.

In contrast we say that the technology exhibits (global) **Nonincreasing Returns to Scale** (NIRS) if

A.10 $\lambda T \subseteq T, 0 \leqq \lambda \leqq 1$.

Constant and nonincreasing returns to scale are general global properties on the technology. Other forms of returns to scale will be introduced which allow the technology to have different returns to scale properties over various ranges of outputs.

The axioms we have introduced here are intended to provide enough structure to create meaningful and useful technologies. In general, we will not impose all of the axioms on a particular technology, rather we will select subsets of these axioms that are suitable for the particular problem under study.

To end this section we connect this general notion of technology and its axioms to the most familiar function representation of technology, namely the production function. By definition, the production function assumes that a single output is produced, i.e., $M = 1$. In this special case we may define a **Production Function** as

$$F(x) = \max\{y : y \in P(x)\}.$$

Since $P(x)$ is a closed and bounded set, the maximum exists, and the function inherits its properties from those of the underlying technology set $P(x)$.

1. The Axiomatic Underpinnings of the Activity Analysis Model

In these essays we make frequent use of the **Activity Analysis Model** as a framework for modeling technology. Given our axiomatic bent, we include an investigation of those properties for this model in this section.[1]

We assume that there are $k = 1, \ldots, K$ activities or observations. These may be various firms or the same firm in different periods, for

[1]The content of this section has also appeared in Färe and Grosskopf (1996). The Activity Analysis Model is the foundation for the DEA (Data Envelopment Analysis) model as formulated in Charnes, Cooper and Rhodes (1978).

example. Each activity is characterized by its input and output vector $(x^k, y^k) = (x_{k1}, \ldots, x_{kN}, y_{k1}, \ldots, y_{kM})$. The coefficients $(x_{kn}, y_{km}), m = 1, \ldots, M, n = 1, \ldots, N, k = 1, \ldots, K$ are required to satisfy certain conditions. These are

i. $x_{kn} \geqq 0, y_{km} \geqq 0, k = 1, \ldots, K, n = 1, \ldots, N,\ m = 1, \ldots, M.$

ii. $\sum_{k=1}^{K} x_{kn} > 0, n = 1, \ldots, N.$

iii. $\sum_{n=1}^{N} x_{kn} > 0, k = 1, \ldots, K.$

iv. $\sum_{k=1}^{K} y_{km} > 0, m = 1, \ldots, M.$

v. $\sum_{m=1}^{M} y_{km} > 0, k = 1, \ldots, K.$

In words, condition i states that inputs and outputs are nonnegative. Condition ii says that each input must be used in at least one observation or activity, and each observation or activity must use at least one input iii. Conditions iv and v mimic conditions ii and iii for outputs. Thus conditions ii-v imply that the matrix of inputs and matrix of outputs have full rank.

The activity analysis model makes use of what are called **Intensity Variables**, $z_k, k = 1, \ldots, K$; one is defined for each activity or observation. These are nonnegative real numbers and their solution values may be interpreted as the extent to which a particular activity or observation is involved in the production of potential outputs. The most basic model, written in terms of an output set is

$$\begin{aligned} P(x) = \{(y_1, \ldots, y_M) : \quad & y_m \leqq \textstyle\sum_{k=1}^{K} z_k y_{km}, & m = 1, \ldots, M, \\ & \textstyle\sum_{k=1}^{K} z_k x_{kn} \leqq x_n, & n = 1, \ldots, N, \\ & z_k \geqq 0, & k = 1, \ldots, K\}. \end{aligned}$$

Next we verify that our activity analysis model satisfies the axioms itemized in the previous section.

A.1 Since $0 \leqq \sum_{k=1}^{K} z_k y_{km}, m = 1, \ldots, M$, the feasibility of zero output given nonzero input holds. If there is zero input, however, nonzero output is not feasible: let $x_n = 0, n = 1, \ldots, N$, then from [ii] and [iii] above, we have $z_k = 0, k = 1, \ldots, K$ and therefore $\sum_{k=1}^{K} z_k y_{km} = 0, m = 1, \ldots, M$; thus only zero output is feasible with zero input.

A.2.S We have already noted that strong disposability of inputs implies weak disposability of inputs. To show that the activity analysis model has freely disposable inputs, we first rewrite it in terms of input sets, i.e.,

$$
\begin{aligned}
L(y) = \{(x_1, \ldots, x_N) : \quad & y_m \leqq \textstyle\sum_{k=1}^{K} z_k y_{km}, & m = 1, \ldots, M, \\
& \textstyle\sum_{k=1}^{K} z_k x_{kn} \leqq x_n, & n = 1, \ldots, N, \\
& z_k \geqq 0, & k = 1, \ldots, K\}.
\end{aligned}
$$

The inequalities in the input constraints yield **A.2.S** for inputs.

A.3.S Similarly, strong disposability of outputs follows from the $m = 1, \ldots, M$ output inequalities.

A.4 To prove that the output sets are bounded, let $x \in \Re_{+}^{N}$. Given that [ii] and [iii] above hold, then the set $Z(x) = \{(z_1, \ldots, z_k) : \sum_{k=1}^{K} z_k x_{kn} \leqq x_n, n = 1, \ldots, N\}$ is bounded and **A.4** holds.

A.5 To show that the graph of technology is closed for our model, first rewrite our activity analysis model in terms of the graph:

$$
\begin{aligned}
T = \{(x, y) : \quad & y_m \leqq \textstyle\sum_{k=1}^{K} z_k y_{km}, & m = 1, \ldots, M, \\
& \textstyle\sum_{k=1}^{K} z_k x_{kn} \leqq x_n, & n = 1, \ldots, N, \\
& z_k \geqq 0, & k = 1, \ldots, K\}.
\end{aligned}
$$

Now let $(x^l, y^l) \to (x^o, y^o)$ and let $(x^l, y^l) \in T$ for all l. Then $y^l \in P(x^l)$ for all l, thus there exist $z^l = (z_1^l, \ldots, z_K^l)$ such that $y_m^l \leqq \sum_{k=1}^{K} z_k^l y_{km}^l$ for all m and $\sum_{k=1}^{K} z_k^l x_{kn}^l \leqq x_n^l$ for all n. Since the input and output constraints are all linear inequalities, it is sufficient to prove that $z^l \to z^o$. Let $\hat{x}_{n^o} = \sup_{l,n}\{x_n^l, n = 1, \ldots, N, l = 1, 2, \ldots\}$. Since x^l converges, $\hat{x}_{n^o}$ is bounded. Define $\hat{x} = (\hat{x}_{1^o}, \ldots, \hat{x}_{N^o})$. From conditions [ii] and [iii] it follows that the set $Z(x)$ in **A.4** is compact and therefore z^l converges.

A.7 To show that the activity analysis model satisfies convexity of the output set, let $y^o, y \in P(x)$, then there are z^o and z such that

$\sum_{k=1}^{K} z_k^o y_{km} \geqq y_m^o, m = 1, \ldots, M$, and $\sum_{k=1}^{K} z_k^o x_{kn} \leqq x_n, n = 1, \ldots, N$,

and

$\sum_{k=1}^{K} z_k y_{km} \geqq y_m, m = 1, \ldots, M$, and $\sum_{k=1}^{K} z_k x_{kn} \leqq x_n, n = 1, \ldots, N$.

Now let $0 \leqq \theta \leqq 1$, then

$\sum_{k=1}^{K}((1-\theta)z_k^o + \theta z_k)y_{km} \geqq (1-\theta)y_m^o + \theta y_m, m = 1, \ldots, M,$

and

$\sum_{k=1}^{K}((1-\theta)z_k^o + \theta z_k)x_{kn} \leqq x_n, n = 1, \ldots, N,$

thus $((1-\theta)y_m^o + \theta y_m) \in P(x)$.

A.6 Like **A.7**.

A.8 Like **A.7**.

A.9 To show that our activity analysis model satisfies constant returns to scale we note that **A.9** is equivalent to

$$P(\lambda x) = \lambda P(x), \lambda > 0.$$

Let $\lambda > 0$, then

$$\begin{aligned} P(\lambda x) &= \{y: \quad y_m \leqq \sum_{k=1}^{K} z_k y_{km}, m = 1, \ldots, M, \\ &\qquad \sum_{k=1}^{K} z_k x_{kn} \leqq \lambda x_n, n = 1, \ldots, N, \\ &\qquad z_k \geqq 0, k = 1, \ldots, K\}. \\ &= \lambda\{(y_m/\lambda): \quad (y_m/\lambda) \leqq \sum_{k=1}^{K}(z_k/\lambda) y_{km}, m = 1, \ldots, M, \end{aligned}$$

$$\begin{aligned} & \sum_{k=1}^{K}(z_k/\lambda)x_{kn} \leqq \lambda x_n/\lambda, n = 1,\ldots,N, \\ & (z_k/\lambda) \geqq 0, k = 1,\ldots,K\} \\ = \quad & \lambda P(x). \end{aligned}$$

If we add the property that $\sum_{k=1}^{K} z_k \leqq 1$ to the output set, then it follows that the technology satisfies **A.10**, i.e., nonincreasing returns to scale. The proof is similar to **A.8** and is omitted.

Finally, under constant returns to scale, by substituting the output inequalities with equalities we get a piecewise linear model that satisfies weak but not necessarily strong disposability of outputs. In a similar way weak input disposability is imposed if the input inequalities are changed to equalities under constant returns to scale. Models with nonconstant returns to scale require nonlinear specifications to accommodate weak disposability; see Essay 2.

[12] Brännlund, R., R. Färe and S. Grosskopf (1998) "Environmental Regulation and Profitability: an application to Swedish paper and pulp mills," *Environmental and Resource Economics* 5, 1-14.

[13] Brännlund, R., Y. Chung, R. Färe and S. Grosskopf (1995), "Emissions Trading and Profitability: the Swedish paper and pulp industry," *Environmental and Resource Economics* 345-356.

[14] Chambers, R. G. (1996) "A New Look at Exact Input, Output, Productivity and Technical Change Measurement," Maryland Agricultural Experiment Station.

[15] Chambers, R. G., Y. Chung and R. Färe, (1998) "Profit, Directional Distance Functions and Nerlovian Efficiency," *Journal of Optimization Theory and Applications* 95:2, 351-364.

[16] Chambers, R., R. Färe and S. Grosskopf (1996) "Productivity Growth in APEC Countries", *Pacific Economic Review* 1:3, 181-190.

[17] Charnes, A. W.W. Cooper and E. Rhodes (1978) "Measuring the Efficiency of Decision Making Units," *European Journal of Operational Research* 2:6, 429-444.

[18] Chung, Y. (1996) *Directional Distance Functions and Undesirable Outputs*, PhD dissertation, Southern Illinois University.

[19] Chung, Y., R. Färe and S. Grosskopf (1997) "Productivity and Undesirable Outputs: A Directional Distance Function Approach," *Journal of Environmental Management* 51, 229-240.

[20] Coase, R. (1960) "The Problem of Social Cost," *The Journal of Law and Economics* 3:1-44.

[21] Cooper, W. W., L.M. Seiford and K. Tone (2000) *Data Envelopment Analysis: A Comprehensive Text with Models, Applications, References and DEA-Solver Software*, Boston: Kluwer Academic Publishers.

[22] Cropper, M. and C. Griffith (1994) "The Interaction of Population Growth and Environmental Quality", *American Economic Association Papers and Proceedings* 84:12, 250-254.

[23] Debreu, G. (1951) "The Coefficient of Resource Utilization," *Econometrica* 19:3, 273-292.

[24] Devaney, M. and W. Weber (2002) "Small Business Lending and Profit Efficiency in Commercial Banking," forthcoming in *Journal of Financial Services Research*.

[25] Diewert, W.E. (1993) "Exact and Superlative Index Numbers," in W. E. Diewert and A.O. Nakamura, eds., *Essays in Index Number Theory* vol. 1, Amsterdam: North-Holland.

[26] Diewert, W.E. (1992) "Fisher Ideal Output, Input and Productivity Indexes Revisited," *Journal of Productivity Analysis* 3:3, 211-248.

[27] Diewert, W.E. (1992) "Fisher Ideal Output, Input and Productivity Indexes Revisited," *Journal of Productivity Analysis* 3:3, 211-248.

[28] Diewert, W.E. (1998) "Index Number Theory Using Differences Rather than Ratios," Department of Economics, UBC, Discussion paper No. 98-10.

[29] Färe, R. (1991) "Measuring Farrell Efficiency for a Firm with Intermediate Inputs", *Academia Economic Papers* 19:2, 329-340.

[30] Färe, R. and S. Grosskopf (1985) "A Nonparametric Cost Approach to Scale Efficiency", *Scandinavian Journal of Economics* 87, 594-604.

[31] Färe, R. and S. Grosskopf (1996) *Intertemporal Production Frontiers: with dynamic DEA*, Boston: Kluwer Academic Publishers.

[32] Färe, R. and S. Grosskopf (1983:a) "Measuring Congestion in Production," *Zeitschrift für Nationalökonomie* 43:3, 257-271.

[33] Färe, R. and S. Grosskopf (1983:b) "Measuring Output Efficiency," *European Journal of Operational Research* 13, 173-179.

[34] Färe, R. and S. Grosskopf (1998) "Shadow Pricing of Good and Bad Commodities," *American Journal of Agricultural Economics* 80, 584-590.

[35] Färe, R. and S. Grosskopf (2000) "Theory and Application of Directional Distance Functions," *Journal of Productivity Analysis* 13, 93-103.

[36] Färe, R., S. Grosskopf and Hernandez-Sancho (2004) "Environmental Performance: An Index Number Approach", *Resource and Energy Economics*, 26:4, 343-352.

[37] Färe, R., S. Grosskopf and C.A.K. Lovell and C. Pasurka (1989) "Multilateral Productivity Comparisons When Some Outputs Are Undesirable," *The Review of Economics and Statistics* 71, 90-98.

[38] Färe, R., S. Grosskopf, C.A.K. Lovell and S. Yaisawarng (1993) "Derivation of Shadow Prices for Undesirable Outputs: A Distance Function Approach," *Review of Economics and Statistics* 75:2, 374-380.

[39] Färe, R., S. Grosskopf and C. Pasurka (1989) "The Effect of Environmental Regulations on the Efficiency of Electric Utilities:1969 Versus 1975", *Applied Economics* 21, 225-235.

[40] Färe, R. S. Grosskopf and W.L. Weber (2001:a) "Shadow Prices of Missouri Public Conservation Land," *Public Finance Review* 29:6, 444-460.

[41] Färe, R. S. Grosskopf and W.L. Weber (2001:b) "Shadow Prices and Pollution Costs in U.S. Agriculture," mimeo.

[42] Färe, R., S. Grosskopf and O. Zaim (2002) "Hyperbolic Efficiency and Return to the Dollar," *European Journal of Operational Research* 136, 671-679.

[43] Färe, R., S. Grosskopf and V. Zelenyuk (2001) "Aggregation of the Nerlovian Profit Indicator," mimeo.

[44] Färe, R. and D. Primont (1995) *Multi-Output Production and Duality: Theory and Applications*, Boston: Kluwer Academic Publishers.

[45] Färe, R., and V. Zelenyuk (2002) "On Mr. Farrell's Decomposition and Aggregation," mimeo.

[46] Färe, R. and G. Whittaker (1996) "Dynamic Measurement of Efficiency: an application to Western public grazing", in *Intertemporal Production Frontiers: with dynamic DEA*, R. Färe and S. Grosskopf, Boston: Kluwer Academic Publishers, 168-186.

[47] Farrell, M.J. (1957) "The Measurement of Productive Efficiency," *Journal of the Royal Statistical Society*, Series A, General 120, Part 3, 253-281.

[48] Fisher, I. (1922) *The Making of Index Numbers*, Boston: Houghton Mifflin.

[49] Fox, K. (1999) "Efficiency at Different Levels ofAggregation: Public vs. Private Sector Firms," *Economics Letters* 65:2, 173-176.

[50] Fukuyama, H. and W. L. Weber (2002) "Estimating Output Allocative Efficiency and Productivity Change: Application to Japanese Banks," *European Journal of Operational Research* 137, 177-190.

[51] Georgescu-Roegen, N. (1951) "The Aggregate Linear Production Function and Its Application to von Neumann's Econmic Model," in T. Koopmans, ed. *Activity Analysis of Production and Allocation*, New York: Wiley.

[52] Grossman, G. M., and A. B. Krueger (1991) "Environmental Impacts of the North American Free Trade Agreement", National Bureau of Economic Research Working Paper 3914, NBER, Cambridge MA.

[53] Grossman, G. M., and A. B. Krueger (1995) "Economic Growth and the Environment", *Quarterly Journal of Economics* 110:2, 353-377.

[54] Holtz-Eakin, D., and T. M. Selden (1995) "Stoking the Fires? CO_2 Emissions and Economic Growth", *Journal of Public Economics* 57 85-101.

[55] Hughes, J. and L. Mester (1998) "Bank Capitalization and Cost: Evidence of Scale Economies in Risk Management and Signaling," *Review of Economics and Statistics* 314-325.

[56] Johansen, L. (1972) *Production Functions*, Amsterdam: North-Holland.

[57] Koopmans, T.C. (1957) *Three Essays on the State of Economic Science*, New York: McGraw-Hill.

[58] Li, S. K. and Y. C. Ng (1995) "Measuring the Productive Efficiency of a Group of Firms," *International Advances in Economic Research* 1:4, 377-390.

[59] Luenberger, D. G. (1992) "Benefit Functions and Duality," *Journal of Mathematical Economics* 21, 461-481.

[60] Luenberger, D. G. (1995) *Microeconomic Theory*, New York: McGraw-Hill.

[61] Mahler, K. (1939) "Ein Übertragungsprinzip für Konvexe Körper," *Casopis pro Pêstovani Matematiky a Fysiky* 4, 93-102.

[62] Malmquist, S. (1953) "Index Numbers and Indifference Surfaces," *Trabajos de Estadistica* 4, 209-242.

[63] Mas-Colell, A., M.D. Whinston and J.R. Green (1995) *Microeconomic Theory* New York: Oxford University Press.

[64] Mattione, R. P. (2000) *Japan: The World's Slowest Crisis, in The Asian Financial Crisis: Lessons for a Resilient Asia* edited by Thye Woo, Jeffrey D. Sachs, and Klaus Schwab.

[65] Maudos, J. and J. M. Pastor (2001) "Cost and Profit Efficiency in Banking: An International Comparison of Europe, Japan, and the USA," *Applied Economics Letters* 8, 383- 387.

[66] Montgomery, J. K. (1929) "Is There a Theoretically Correct Price Index of a Group of Commodities?" Rome: Roma L'Universale Tipogr. Poliglotta.

[67] Montgomery, J. K. (1937) *The Mathematical Problem of the Price Index*, Orchard House, Westminister: P. S. King and Son.

[68] Nerlove, M. (1965) *Esimation and Identification of Cobb-Douglas Production Functions*, Princeton: Princeton University Press.

[69] Panayotou, T. (1993) "Empirical Tests and Policy Analysis of Environmental Degradation at Different Stages of Economic Development," Working Paper WP238, Technology and Employment Programme, International Labor Office, Geneva.

[70] Peek, J. and E. S. Rosengren (1997) "The International Transmission of Financial Shocks: The Case of Japan," *The American Economic Review* 87:4, 495-505.

[71] Peek, Joe and Eric S. Rosengren (2000) "Collateral Damage: Effects of the Japanese bank Crisis on Real Activity in the United States," *The American Economic Review* 90:1, 30-45.

[72] Pittman, R.W. (1981) "Issue in Pollution Control: Interplant Cost Differences and Economies of Scale," *Land Economics* 57:1, 1-17.

[73] Saunders, A. and I. Walter (1994) *Universal Banking in the United States: What Could we Gain? What Could We Lose?*, Oxford: Oxford University Press.

[74] Sealey, C. W., and J.T. Lindley (1977) "Inputs, Outputs, and a Theory of Production and Cost at Depository Institutions" *Journal of Finance* 32, 1267-1282.

[75] Selden, T., and D. Song (1994) "Environmental Quality and Development: Is There a Kuznets Curve for Air Pollution Emissions?", *Journal of Environmental Economics and Management* 27, 147-162.

[76] Shafik, N. and S. Bandyoypadhyay (1992) "Economic Growth and Environmental Quality: Time Series and Cross Country Evidence", World Bank Policy Research Working Paper, WPS 904, World Bank, Washington D.C. (1992).

[77] Shephard, R.W. (1953) *Cost and Production Functions*, Princeton: Princeton University Press.

[78] Shephard, R.W. (1970) *Theory of Cost and Production Functions*, Princeton: Princeton University Press.

[79] Shephard, R.W. (1974) *Indirect Production Functions*, Meisenheim am Glan: Verlag Anton Hain.

[80] Shephard, R.W. and R. Färe (1974) "The Law of Diminishing Returns," *Zeitschrift für Nationalökonomie* 34, 69-90.

[81] Summers, R. and A. Heston (1991) "The Penn World Table (Mark 5): An Expanded Set of International Comparisons, 1950-1988", *Quarterly Journal of Economics* 106:2, 327-68.

[82] Taskin, F. and O. Zaim (2000) "Searching for a Kuznets Curve in Environmental Efficiency Using Kernel Estimation", *Economics Letters* 68, 217-1223.

[83] Tyteca, D. (1996) "On The Measurement Of Environmental Performance of Firms—A Literature Review and a Productive Efficiency Perspective," *Journal of Environmental Management* 46, 281-308.

[84] Varian, H. (1992) *Microeconomic Analysis*, 3rd ed., New York: W.W. Norton and Company.

[85] Ylvinger, S. (2000) "Industry Performance and Structural Efficiency Measures: Solutions to Problems in Firm Models," *European Journal of Operational Research* 121, 164-174.

[86] Zaim, O. and F. Taskin (2000) "A Kuznets Curve in Environmental Efficiency: An Application on OECD Countries", in *Environmental and Resource Economics* 17, 21-36.

Topic Index

Activity Analysis Model
axioms, 157
Aggregate Farrell Input Index of Technical Efficiency, 124
Aggregate indication axiom, 115
Aggregating the output and input oriented Farrell efficiency indexes, 115
Aggregation across inputs and outputs, 120
Aggregation and decompositions, 131
Aggregation of any possible input and output vector, 104
Aggregation of efficiency and productivity, 93
Aggregation of output oriented Farrell Indexes, 117
Aggregation of technical efficiency, 102, 116, 120
Aggregation of the cost efficiency indicator, 108
Aggregation of the Farrell cost efficiency index, 118
Aggregation of the revenue and cost indicators, 105
Allocative efficiency, 8, 13, 19, 22, 25
Allocative efficiency, 29
Allocative efficiency, 123, 127
Axiom of Aggregate Indication, 102
Axioms of production, 151
Axioms of Production, **153**
Bads as an 'intermediate' input, 75
Base invariance of the distance function, 59
Biomass, 70
Common-pool resource, 65, 70, 75
Constant returns to scale, 21–22, 156
Convexity, 155
Cost Aggregated Directional Input Distance Function, 126
Cost aggregated efficiency, 123
Cost aggregation, 124
Cost efficiency, 26–27
Cost efficiency indicator, **22**, 25–26
Cost efficient, **24**
Cost function, **23**, 31
properties, 23
Cost Minimization, ix, 23
Cost version of Koopmans' theorem, 99–**100**
Decomposition of the Revenue Indicator, ix, 20
Direction-Efficient, **9**
Direction-Efficient, **17**
Direction-efficient, 17–18
Direction vector g_y, 21
Directional distance function, **6**–8, xiii, 19, 38, 63, 107
directional output distance function, **16**
estimation, 12
Directional Input Distance Function, **24**
Directional input distance function, 24–25, 36
properties, 24
Directional input vector, 22
Directional output distance function, 16–17, 32, 35, 53, 55, **61**, 112
Directional output distance function with good and bad outputs, ix, 54
Directional output vector, 15, 35
Directional Technology Distance Function, 6, ix
Directional technology distance function, **35**, **136**, 138
Directional vector, 5, 35, 55
Distance functions
directional distance function, **6**, xiii
directional output distance function, **16**
input distance function, xiii
output distance function, xiii
Downstream firm, 73
Downstream technology, 68

Efficiency and Direction Vectors, 10, ix
Efficiency change, 54
Efficiency indexes, 27
Efficient subset, 5, 18
Environmental Kuznets Curve, 77, 85
Environmental Performance Index, **58**
Environmental performance index, 78, **81**, 84
Externalities, 65
Farrell cost efficiency index, 123
Farrell Index of Allocative Efficiency, 33
Farrell Index of Cost Efficiency, 29
Farrell Index of Revenue Efficiency, 33
Farrell Index of Technical Efficiency, 29, 33
Farrell Index Unbiased Input Aggregation, 125
Farrell index unbiased output aggregation, 129
Farrell industry index of cost efficiency, 118
Farrell industry index of technical efficiency, 116
Farrell Input-Oriented Efficiency Indexes, ix, 29
Farrell Output Oriented Efficiency Indexes, ix, 34
Farrell Output Subvector Index of Technical Efficiency, **128**
Farrell revenue efficiency, 116
Farrell Subvector Index of Technical Efficiency, 124
Farrell technical efficiency, 34
Farrell technical efficiency indexes, 121
Firm aggregation results, 104
Firm allocative efficiency, 117
Firm profit function, **97**
Firm specific inputs, 114
Fisher tests, 57, 81
Fixed effects model, 87
Fox Paradox, **94**
Fox paradox, 115
Good quantity index, **81**
Hausman test, 87
Homogeneity, 8
Hyperbolic allocative efficiency, 41
Hyperbolic distance function, 41
Index, 1, 35
Index of bad outputs, 81
Indication property, 30
Indication Property, 33
Indicator, 1
Indicator unbiased input aggregation, 127
Indicator unbiased output aggregation, 130
Indicators, 35
Individual quota, 76
Industry allocative efficiency, 102, **117**, 119, 138
Industry allocative input efficiency, 109
Industry cost efficiency index, 118
Industry cost efficiency indicator, 109
Industry directional technology distance function, 102, 119
Industry distance function, 107
Industry efficiency, 133
Industry index of technical efficiency, 118
Industry indicator, 100
Industry input requirement set, **99**
Industry input vector, 108
Industry output distance function, 108, **116**
Industry output set, **98**
Industry profit function, **97**, 101, 138
Industry profit indicator, 102
Industry revenue efficiency index, 132
Industry revenue function, **105**, 115
Industry revenue indicator, 106
Industry technical efficiency, 102, 138
Industry technical efficiency indicator, 108
Industry technical input efficiency indicator, 109
Industry technology, **96**, 103
Input Aggregation, ix, 123
Input Correspondence, 152
Input Distance Function, ix
Input distance function, **27**
Input Distance Function, 28
Input distance function, 41
  properties, **27**
Input isoquant, **30**
Input requirement set, 30, 36
Input Requirement Sets, 152
Japanese banking industry, 133
Japanese Banking System, 134
Johansen firm and industry production, ix, 112
Johansen industry model, 111
Koopmans' Theorem, ix
Koopmans' theorem, **97**
Koopmans' Theorem, 98
Luenberger Productivity Indicator, **53**
Luenberger productivity indicator, 54, **119**
Luenberger profitability change indicator, 139
Mahler Inequality, 28, 32
Mahler inequality, 37
Maximum revenue, 21
Nerlovian Industry Profit Indicator, **101**
Nerlovian profit efficiency, 26, 138
Nerlovian profit indicator, 2
Nerlovian Profit Indicator, **5**
Nerlovian profit indicator, 8, 13, 96
Nerlovian Profit Indicator, 101
Network DEA, 65
Network model, 67, 75
Network technology, 69
Nonincreasing returns to scale, **157**

Null-joint, 67
Null-jointness, **46**, 51–52, 57
Null-jointness, 80, 83
Null-jointness, 90
Null jointness, 49
Observed cost, **22**
Optimal 'catch', 76
Output Correspondence, 152
Output distance function, 31–33
  properties, 31
Output distance functions, xiii
Output index of allocative efficiency, 129
Output isoquant, **18**, **33**
Output set, 31, 49
Output sets, 13, 20
Price aggregation, 120
Production function, 32, 107, 157
Profit efficiency, 39
Profit efficient, **5**
Profit estimation, 12
Profit function, **3**–**4**, 39, 137
Profit maximization, 75
Profit maximization model, 71
Profit with the network technology, 74
Proof of Cost Corollary, 148
Proof of Revenue Corollary, 148
Properties of the directional output distance function, 16
Properties of the distance function, **9**
Property rights, 65
Property rights and profitability, 65
Quadratic directional distance function, 64
Quadratic function, 63
Quantity index, 56
Quantity index of bad outputs, **57**, 79
Quantity index of good outputs, 79
Random effects model, 87
Representation property, 9
Return to the dollar, 41–42
Returns to scale, 156
Revenue Aggregate Farrell Output Index of Technical Efficiency, 129
Revenue Corollary to Koopmans' Theorem, 99
Revenue efficiency, 19, 33, 115
Revenue efficiency indicator, **15**, 19–20, 26
Revenue function, **14**, 32, **61**, **98**
  properties, 14
Revenue Maximization, ix, 14
Risk-based capital requirement, 135
Shadow price, 61
Shadow prices, 61, 64
Shephard output distance function, 35
Single output industry production model, 110
Strong disposability of inputs, 22, 154
Strong disposability of outputs, 22, **47**, 154
Subvector cost efficiency decomposition, 126
Subvector Cost Efficiency Indicator, **127**
Subvector Cost Function, **125**
Subvector Directional Input Distance Function, 126
Subvector directional output distance function, 131
Subvector distance function, 57
Subvector Input Allocative Efficiency, 126
Subvector output distance function, 80
Törnqvist index, 60
Technical change, 54
Technical efficiency, 8–9, 12, 16, 19, 21, 24–25, 30, 34, 107
Technical efficiency indicators, 121
Technical inefficiency, 42
Technology, **3**, 70
Technology, 151
Technology efficient, **5**
Technology
  output sets, 13
The Directional Input Distance Function, ix, 37
The Directional Output Distance Function, ix, 17
The Network Model with Externality, ix, 66
The Revenue Aggregation Theorem, ix, 99
The Technology Hyperbolic Distance Function, ix, 40
Translation property, **8**, 17, 56, 63, 105, 112
Undesirable outputs, 46
Undesirables as inputs, 49
Upstream firm's profit, 71
Upstream technology, 68
Variable returns to scale, 21, 51
Weak and Strong Disposability of Outputs, ix, 48
Weak disposability, 49, 52, 57, 68, 83, 90
Weak disposability of inputs, **67**, **154**
Weak disposability of outputs, 46–**47**, 51
Weak disposability of outputs, 80

Author Index

Aczél, J., 95, 104, 132
Aigner, D., 64
Allais, M., 42
Balk, B., xii, 42, 147
Ball, E., 91
Bandyopadhyay, S., 78
Bennet, T., 1
Berger, A., 133
Blackorby, C., 93, 102, 105, 109, 115, 133
Brännlund, R., 75, 91
Chambers, R., 42, 53–54, 77, 91
Charnes, A., 65, 157
Chung, Y., 42, 75, 91
Chu, S., 64
Coase, R., 65
Cooper, W.W., 42, 65, 157
Cropper, M., 78
Debreu, G., 42
Devaney, M., 135
Diewert, W.E., 1, 42, 59, 81–82
Farrell, M., 27, 42
Fisher, I., 57, 81
Fox, K., 94, 147
Fukuyama, H., xi, 133
Färe, R., 42, 54, 58, 65–66, 75, 77–78, 81, 90–91, 135, 139, 147, 151, 157
Georgescu-Roegen, N., 41
Grifell-Tatjė, E., xi
Griffith, C., 78
Grosskopf, 147
Grosskopf, S., 42, 54, 58, 65–66, 75, 77–78, 81, 84, 90–91, 135, 139, 151, 157
Grossman, G., 77, 90
Hernandez-Sancho, F., 58, 79, 81, 84
Holtz-Eakin, D., 78
Hughes, J., 135
Humphrey, D., 133
Johansen, L., 110
Koopmans, T., 96, 138
Kreuger, A., 77
Krueger, A., 90
Lee, W.F., xi, 65, 91
Li, S.K.K., 117
Logan, J., xi
Lovell, C.A.K., 42, 79, 90
Luenberger, D., 42, 147
Mahler, K., 27, 42
Malmquist, S., 42, 80
Mas-Colell, A., 147
Mattione, R., 134
Maudos, J., 142
Mester, L., 135
Montgomery, J., 1
Nehring, R., 91
Nerlove, M., 42
Ng, Y., 117
Panayotou, T., 90
Pastor, J., 104, 142
Pasurka, C., 42, 78, 90
Peek, J., 135
Primont, D., 93, 147, 151
Rhodes, E., 65, 157
Rosengren, E., 135
Russell, R.R., 93, 102, 105, 109, 115, 133
Saunders, A., 134
Seiford, L., 42
Selden, T., 78, 90
Shafik, N., 78
Shephard, R.W., 27, 42, 66, 90, 151
Song, D., 78, 90
Taskin, F., 79
Tone, K., 42
Tyteca, D., 79
Törnqvist, L., 60
Walter, I., 134
Weber, W., xi, 91, 133, 135
Whittaker, G., 77
Yaisawarng, S., 91
Ylvinger, S., 133

Zaim, O., xi, 42, 77, 79
Zelenyuk, V., 147